Mountain Biking UK

GRIME TIME

Mountain Biking UK

GRIME TIME

The Complete Guide to Mountain Bike Maintenance and Repair

Paul Smith

future BOOKS

First published in 1994 by
Future Books
a division of Future Publishing Limited
Beauford Court, 30 Monmouth Street, Bath BA1 2BW

Text copyright © Paul Smith 1994
Photographs © Future Publishing unless otherwise indicated on page 144
First Edition 1994
Reprinted 1995

Designed by Maria Bowers

A CIP catalogue record for this book is available from the British Library
ISBN: 1 85981 025X

Printed and bound by Ebenezer Baylis

2 4 6 8 10 9 7 5 3 1

If you would like more information on our other cycling titles please write to
The Publisher, Future Books at the above address

GRIME TIME

Contents

Welcome to grime time

Mountain biking, by its very nature, abuses the structures and systems that make up a bike. Because of this, those systems will quickly wear out if you don't maintain them on a regular basis. So to get the most mileage out of a component it pays to keep it in good working order. It's not difficult, but it can be time and money consuming.

Cleaning a bike after a muddy ride will help guard against the dried dirt getting rubbed into the working parts of the bike the next time you use it. A couple of buckets of water, a stiff brush, and a water-dispersing lubricant is all you need. A garden hose is OK as long as you don't spray directly against the seals of bearings such as hubs, bottom bracket, and headset. It also helps if you try not to spray water near the sections of frame where the seat post and handlebar stem are inserted because water can find its way into the frame and cause corrosion – not just of the frame, but of the parts that fit into it. A quick squirt of water-dispersing lube in key areas like the chain, down the seat tube, up the steerer tube, along exposed lengths of cables, etc., will see that corrosion doesn't set in.

Regular cleaning and lubrication is the key to long term serviceability – neglect the bike and it will cost you more in the long run. Maintenance should become a natural part of using your bike. Just as you would automatically put a helmet on before riding, it soon becomes second nature to clean and lube the chain once a week, check the brake blocks and cables, and give everything a wipe down after a ride.

Eventually you'll find you begin to clean and lube everything on a more frequent basis, you'll buy silicon polish for the paint, metal polish for the bare alloy parts, specific lubes and greases for specific parts... Bike maintenance can get obsessive, but the only harm you can do is get a sore finger from all that polishing! It's a good feeling to sit back, after a couple of hours tweaking, and know that your bike is spot on,

JARGON

BOTTOM BRACKET – the bearing and axle assembly in the frame which the crank assembly fastens to.

BRAKES – the system that slows/stops the bike. Usually when you pull a handlebar-mounted lever. These must be kept in 100 per cent tip-top condition for the bike to be safe to ride.

BRAKE BLOCKS – the rubber pads that locate into the brake and press against the wheel rim when you pull the brake lever.

CABLES – the wire system used to operate brakes and gears. Consisting of an inner section which is pulled (tension), and an outer section which is squeezed (compressed). Both inner and outer must be in good condition to operate under tension and compression.

HEADSET – the bearing assembly between the fork steerer and the headtube of the frame.

HUB – the unit at the centre of the wheel. It houses the wheel bearings and provides for spoke location via the flanges.

LUBE/LUBRICANT, WET AND DRY – wet lubes stay wet to the touch when applied. Dry lubes evaporate to leave a dry film (usually teflon based). Wet lubes are good for wet conditions, while dry lubes are good for dusty conditions because they don't attract dirt.

SEAT POST – the post that fits into the seat tube of the frame and has the seat fastened to the top of it.

SEAT TUBE – the part of the frame that the seat post fits into.

STEERER TUBE – the tube coming from the forks that runs up inside the headtube of the frame.

with nothing bent or broken, no frayed cables, no dirt in the chain, and all the paint covered in a protective layer of polish.

Hopefully this book will show you, in an easy, step-by-step way, how to service your bike and explain technical terms as we go along. If you think the job is going to be too difficult, try enlisting the help of a more knowledgeable friend. Not necessarily a biker – anyone with an understanding of mechanical gizmos should be able to help. It might even be best to hand them this book first and show them what you are trying to do.

While preparing this book I discovered that most people had a fear of taking things apart. Yet as soon as a part was stripped and they could see the various bits, they quickly understood how it worked and its relationship to the rest of the bike. The hardest part was getting them to dismantle the thing in the first place – but once they'd done that, they became more confident.

Another problem – for me this time – is the constant development of the design, technology and manufacture of mountain bikes. This means parts are being changed and improved year by year, so writing a maintenance book is a battle of compromise between catering for old and new equipment. The one golden rule of servicing equipment is this…

Controlled explosion

If it is in working order, but just needs a service, disassemble it and lay all of the parts out in the order in which they were removed – to form a kind of three dimensional exploded diagram. Clean the parts one by one, transferring them to a clean area as you do. Reassembly is then a simple matter of joining together the 'exploded' components in the reverse order.

I use this technique quite often, in fact while writing the book I stripped and rebuilt a malfunctioning Shimano Rapid Fire gear shifter unit. I had no idea what the current Rapid Fire shifters were like – I'd never seen inside one before – but after a couple of hours it was back together and working better than ever.

Bikes are fairly simple things once you begin to understand how all the bits work and, with the help of this book, you should soon be able to strip and service your bike with complete confidence.

I also hope that even the more experienced among you will find a few useful hints and tips – unless you've built an entire bike from scratch, there are bound to be a few gaps in your knowledge. And of course if there is anything that still seems confusing – or you know a better way of doing something – don't hesitate to let me know…

ANATOMY OF THE BIKE

A Rear Sprockets

B Rear dropout

C Rear mech

D Front Mech

E Chainset and behind bottom bracket

F Stem

G Brake and gear levers

H Headset

I Front cantilever brake

J Front dropout

K Rear cantilever brake

Anatomy of the bike

TOOL KIT

THE RIGHT TOOLS FOR THE JOB

You only need a handful of special tools to maintain and adjust the various parts on a mountain bike, the rest being common to any other bicycle. But first, a little on the subject of buying tools.

Before journalism, photography, and mountain bikes became my job I spent a few years as an apprentice Cosworth technician, then as a fully qualified Alfa Romeo technician, while at the same time studying the design and manufacture of light vehicle (cars and motorcycles) chassis/suspension.

During this time I came to learn the importance of having the correct tools for the job, and knowing how to use those tools. High quality tools, such as Snap On and Blue Point, are fine when you are using them on a day-to-day basis is, but for everyday use on mountain bikes the tools from your local motoring accessory shop are perfectly adequate.

Once you've got your tools it pays to keep them clean and organised. Small plastic tool boxes are OK, but a good tool roll is better (heavy duty cloth or leather ones are the best). With a tool box you often have to dig around to find what you want, and dirt, water, oil and grease will soon build up in the tool box and the tools will suffer. Also with a tool roll you soon get into the habit of wiping them down before you put them back into their pockets.

A good compromise is to put a couple of tool rolls in a tool box. Then you can use the extra compartments of the box for small spare parts like cables, brake blocks, nuts and bolts, etc.

For a more comprehensive collection of tools, try a tool board. Take a sheet of plywood, lay all the tools out in a sensible pattern, then fasten them to the board with clips or hang them from nails. Then draw an outline of the tool on the board and label its position, so you always put it back in the right place.

Simple Dos and Don'ts

You've got your tools, they're clean and well-organised, and you know how to use them right? Maybe not... Here are a few simple guidelines that are often overlooked.

1 When using a knife never cut towards yourself. Always cut in such a way that a slip will send the blade away from you and your hands.

2 Never push away from yourself when using a spanner, Allen key or ratchet. If it slips you'll end up hitting your hand on whatever lies in your path, and usually there's something sharp in the way. If at all possible, always pull towards yourself when tightening or loosening something.

3 When pushing a screwdriver against a screw, never put a hand behind the screw. If the screwdriver slips you'll stab yourself.

4 When using wire cutters to trim a cable, either cover the cable with a cloth, to stop pieces flying off, or wear eye protection (preferably both). A flying piece of wire can blind, so don't risk it – use caution for your own and other people's safety.

5 After using a saw or a file don't blow away the shavings. A piece of debris can permanently damage an eye. Wear eye protection and use a small brush to remove any shavings.

6 Whenever possible use the ring end of a spanner or a socket. The open end of a spanner is designed to be used when access to the bolt or nut is limited, it is not designed to take full tightening loads. In addition to this the open end of a spanner will only apply the force at two points, and this increases the chance of damaging the bolt or nut. A ring spanner or socket spreads the load over six points, which means less damage to the fastener and less chance of the spanner or socket slipping off.

JARGON

ALLEN KEY – hexagonal-shaped rod bent at 90° that fits into the head of an Allen bolt. Almost every bike uses Allen bolts.

BOTTOM BRACKET – the bearing and axle assembly in the frame which the crank assembly fastens to.

CABLES – the wire system used to operate brakes and gears. Consisting of an inner section which is pulled (tension), and an outer section which is squeezed (compressed). Both inner and outer must be in good condition to operate under tension and compression.

CONE – the cone shaped part of a bearing assembly. Used with a cup and bearings.

CHAIN WHIP – tool used to hold the rear gear sprockets while the lockring or threaded sprocket are removed.

CRANK EXTRACTOR – tool used to remove crank arms.

DEGREASER – solvent which will remove grease. Useful for cleaning components, especially the chain when used with a chain cleaning tool.

⇨

HEADSET – the bearing assembly between the fork steerer and the headtube of the frame.

LUBE/LUBRICANT, WET AND DRY – wet lubes stay wet to the touch when applied. Dry lubes evaporate to leave a dry film (usually teflon based). Wet lubes are good for wet conditions, while dry lubes are good for dusty conditions because they don't attract dirt.

HYPERGLIDE – the brand name given to Shimano rear gear sprockets that have profiled teeth and special 'shift ramps'.

SPOKE KEY – tool for turning the spoke nipples of a wheel so that the spoke tension can be adjusted.

With care, thought and the right technique, you can avoid workshop injury and stress.

The tools you'll need

For general weekly maintenance, the following list will do the job:

- **2, 2.5, 3, 4, 5, 6 and 8mm Allen keys**
- **8, 9, 10, 11mm spanners (combination – open end and ring)**
- **Phillips No 2 screwdriver**
- **Small pliers**
- **Cable cutters (it's worth buying high quality cutters)**
- **Chain tool (to suit narrow chains)**
- **Two tyre levers**
- **Puncture kit**
- **Pump**
- **Chain cleaning tool**
- **Degreaser**
- **Chain lubricant**
- **Grease**

This will allow you to adjust brake and gear systems, replace cables, change tyres and tubes, adjust bars and stem, seat and post, clean the chain, and fit new brake pads. It's a good basic tool kit for tackling straightforward maintenance – leave the more complicated bottom bracket, headset and wheel jobs to your local bike shop.

More tools you'll need

For a full service tool kit you'll need all of the tools on page 14 plus...

- Two headset spanners (32mm for 1 inch, 36mm for 1 1/8 inch or 40mm for 1 1/4 inch)
- Bottom bracket spanners (or Shimano tool TL-UN52 for Shimano sealed BB's)
- Cone spanners
- 15mm pedal spanner
- Crank extractor
- Chain whips
- Freewheel or Hyperglide lockring tool
- 10mm Allen key (for Shimano freehub)
- Spoke key
- Chainring bolt tool (Shimano TL-FC20)
- Brushes (tooth brush, stiff cleaning brush, etc.)
- Files (small 2nd cut round)
- Medium vice with soft jaws

In addition you may want to include a work stand, a wheel-trueing stand, a wheel dishing tool, and a headset pressing tool. Your tool kit would then be as good, if not better, than those of most bike shop mechanics! It would allow you to do just about every job on a mountain bike apart from frame repairs – and they should really be left to a reputable frame builder or repairer anyway.

Use the right specialist tool for the job. From top: spoke key, bottom bracket lock ring adjustable, crank puller, wire cutters, cone spanners, headset/pedal spanner, headset lockring spanner.

TYRES AND TUBES

Introduction

Repairing an inner tube used to be a stop-gap measure until the tube could be replaced with a new one. But advances in glue technology and patch design mean a repaired tube can now be used with complete confidence until the next puncture, and so on, until the inner tube weighs too much or starts to deform because of all the patches!

Getting a puncture is a hassle, so it's best to carry a spare tube when you're out riding – then all you have to do is fit the new tube (see 'Fixing a flat fast' on page 24) and stuff the old one in your bum bag or whatever, to be fixed when you get home. Fixing a puncture out on the trail is horrible, especially when it's raining and cold. Once you get home, though, you can take your time and fix the tube correctly.

Puncture kits vary in quality, and if yours includes that useless bit of sandpaper, chuck it in the bin and replace it with medium-grade emery cloth – it works better and lasts longer. Go for a puncture kit with thin-edged patches (usually a different coloured edge), these are the best. Rema Tip Top make by far the best puncture kits, and the smallest of their range are excellent value for money as well as a small handy size (a bit bigger than a matchbox).

Punctures come in two types, fast or slow, and the slow ones can be a nightmare to locate – especially those where it takes a week for the tyre to lose air. Fast punctures are usually caused by the rim pinching the inner tube as you ride over and into rocks and such like. They leave two small (or big depending how fast you're going) cuts either side of the inner tube, and are often referred to as 'snakebites' punctures. A front wheel blow out can cause a critical loss of control and a nasty crash, so always keep your tyres inflated correctly.

Tyres and tubes

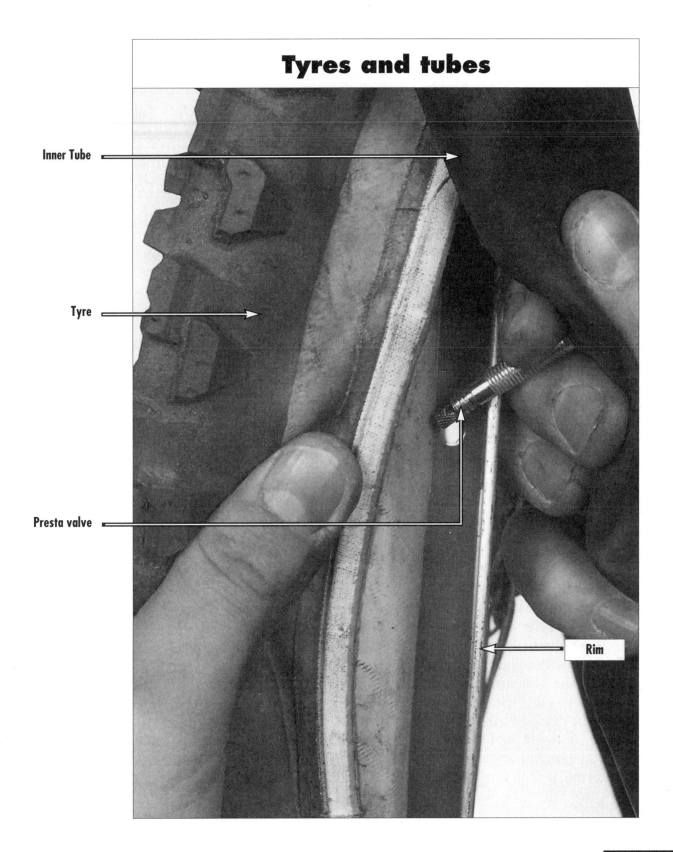

Inner Tube

Tyre

Presta valve

Rim

1 Unless the hole is so big it's easy to find, your first step is to inflate the tube. This enables you to find the hole(s) by simply listening to where the air is coming from. With slow, hard-to-find punctures, it often pays to inflate the tube until it doubles in size and then dunk it in a bowl of water. As soon as the hole goes under the water a stream of air bubbles will show where it is.

2 Shown here is a typical thorn-type puncture, a very small hole that requires only a small patch. Bigger holes or cuts will need bigger patches. If there are two holes close to each other but the largest patch you have only just covers them, it's better to use two small ones. The closer the hole is to the edge of the patch the more likely it is that the patch will leak.

3 Mark around the hole with either the strange yellow wax provided in the puncture kit and roughen it up with the emery cloth, or stick a bit of electrical tape over the hole so you know exactly where it is. Once you've marked the hole, deflate the tube.

4 Wrap the deflated tube around the back of your hand and roughen the area around the hole with emery cloth. Start at the hole and work outwards to create an area twice the size of the patch – that way you know the hole is right in the centre of the rough area and you know where to place the patch. Roughening the tube like this gets rid of any ridges that might have been left when the tube was manufactured and also provides a key for the glue which will work better on rough surfaces.

5 Apply glue to the rough area and spread it out thinly with either your fingers or the end of the tube of glue. Keep an eye on the location of the hole when it disappears as you spread the glue.

6 Wait at least two minutes for the glue to dry. Vulcanising glue works like a contact adhesive. The glue on the patch reacts with the glue on the tube and they stick together, but for this reaction to work properly the glue on the tube must be left to dry for a while – the instructions with the repair kit will say how long.

7 Remove the foil backing from the patch, making sure you keep the glued surface of the patch clean. It won't work if you get dirt, water, or sweat on it.

8 Stick the patch over the hole. If you've kept an eye on the location of the hole, the patch should be right over the top of it, with the hole in the centre.

9 Press firmly on the patch, starting from the centre outwards. If you now trap the tube under a stack of books, while you clean the rim and check the inside of the tyre for thorns and so on, you will ensure that a constant pressure is applied to the patch while the glue is curing.

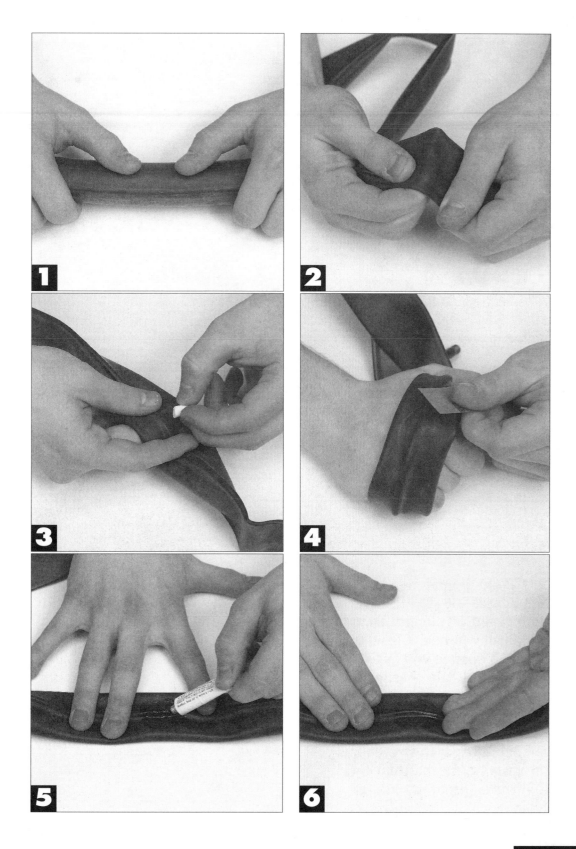

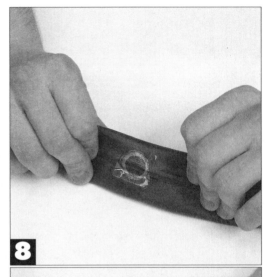

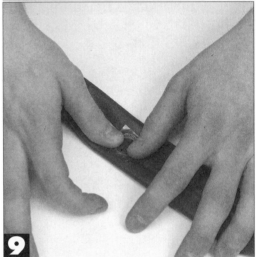

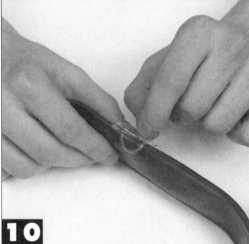

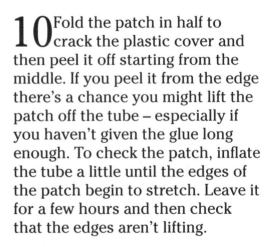

JARGON

SNAKEBITE PUNCTURES – when the tyre squashes enough so that the wheel rim pinches the inner tube and splits it. Usually caused by running too low a tyre pressure.

10 Fold the patch in half to crack the plastic cover and then peel it off starting from the middle. If you peel it from the edge there's a chance you might lift the patch off the tube – especially if you haven't given the glue long enough. To check the patch, inflate the tube a little until the edges of the patch begin to stretch. Leave it for a few hours and then check that the edges aren't lifting.

If all is well, deflate the tube and use it as a spare – or refit it into the tyre, inflate, and go ride.

Hints 'n' tips

Schrader valve

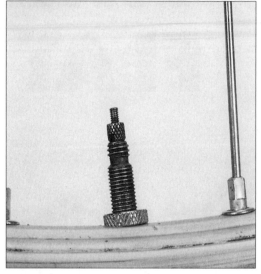

Presta valve

Chalk

Those funny little square lumps of chalk that are supplied with puncture repair kits come in handy if you are installing a freshly-repaired tube into a tyre. Rub the chalk on to the emery cloth and then tap the chalk dust from the emery cloth on to any excess glue around the patch. This prevents the inner tube sticking to the inside of the tyre when inflated.

Carry a cloth

Fixing a puncture when you're out riding is not the best option, but if you don't have a spare tube it's all you can do. It pays to carry a cloth with you to wipe a wet or muddy tube after you've found the hole. If it's raining, wait until you're ready to apply the glue before you dry the tube, that way there's less chance of water contaminating the glue. Wrap your puncture kit in the cloth, secure it with elastic bands, and stick it in your bum bag, pocket, Camelback or under your seat (wrapped in a plastic bag).

Patches

You can buy patches separately, which is advisable because a small tube of glue will often do three times the number of patches supplied with a repair kit.

FIXING A FLAT FAST

Introduction

If you get a puncture when you're out riding it's a pain. Getting a puncture in a race is even worse. Fumbling around at the side of the course while your fellow competitors trundle past is not the best feeling in the world, and having your riding buddies hang around watching while you patch up a tube isn't the best way of maintaining good friendships. How about a little help, guys?

Don't bother trying to fix a punctured tube on the spot if you can avoid it, always carry a spare tube with you and take the punctured one home and fix it there. That doesn't mean you don't carry a puncture kit, because if you puncture again and nobody has a spare tube you'll have to use it.

There are a few ways to get a tyre off, either with your bare hands (all down to rim and tyre choice), with one tyre lever, or with two tyre levers. Once the tube is out you can check the tyre for whatever caused the puncture, put in the new tube, inflate and go.

Releasing the straddle wire of the brake in order to remove the wheel.

Removing a tyre with bare hands or just one tyre lever

1 After removing the wheel, deflate the tyre if it isn't totally flat already. Put the dust cap and lockring (for Presta valves) where you know where to find them. Put them with the new tube or better still with the pump. It's all too easy to lose a small dust cap in the grass and you don't want to be wasting time looking for it. Push the valve up inside the tyre to unseat the tube from between the tyre beads.

2 Hold the wheel up in the air with one hand grabbing the tyre, and then work around the tyre with the other hand pushing the sidewalls inwards. This lets the wheel drop down as the bead of the tyre is pushed into the well of the rim. After one complete revolution with the bead-pinching hand there should be enough slack tyre in the stationary hand to enable you to pull the tyre off the rim. If it's still tight you can try again, but this time stand on the bottom of the rim with your foot and pull upwards on the top of the tyre as you work around the rim pushing the bead into the well again.

If that doesn't work, you'll have to use a tyre lever.

3 Insert the tyre lever under the bead of the tyre and lever it all of the way into the spokes. If you are racing you won't worry about pinching the tube with the lever - especially if you are racing – you just want to get the tube out as fast as possible.

With tight tyre and rim combinations this is sometimes impossible, and you will need two tyre levers (see page 28).

4 Push the tyre lever around the rim unseating the rest of the bead. If the tyre lever is too tight to push then trap the removed section of bead with one hand, remove the tyre lever, and repeat the process two or three inches along the rim until enough of the bead is removed to allow you to pull the tyre off with your hands.

With practice the act of removing the wheel, collecting the slack in the tyre and pulling it off the rim becomes one long movement. I've seen top racers get the tube out of a tyre less than fifteen seconds after stopping the bike!

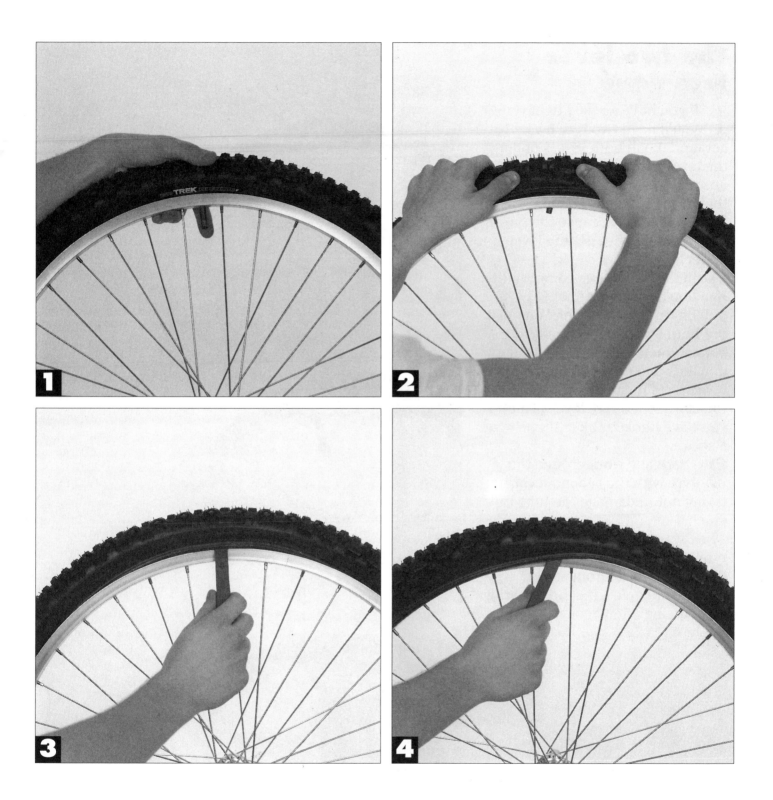

The two lever technique

1 If you have a really tight tyre you'll need two tyre levers to get it off. Push both levers under the tyre's bead roughly six inches apart. Don't lever the first one and then try and get the second one under the bead because the tyre will be too tight to get the lever under it.

2 Pull the first lever down until it hooks around a spoke. Then pull on the second lever. You must put both levers under the tyre before you try and lift the bead upwards and over the rim. With some tyres it can be very difficult to get a second tyre lever in after you have hooked the first one over a spoke.

3 Gradually work around the tyre with the second lever, trying not to damage the tube too much.

   Really tight tyres may need three tyre levers! If this is the case take the tyre off away from easily offended people – mucho swearing and cursing often ensues.

Changing the tube

1 Once one side of the tyre is off the rim, reach in and pull out the inner tube. Pull the tyre open and look inside for anything protruding from the inner surface of the tyre.

2 Inflate the tube until it stays in shape. Only put enough air in to stop it flopping around – this will make it much easier to fit into the tyre.

3 Push the valve through the hole in the rim and push the rest of the tube into the tyre. Try to push the tube well into the rim so that it won't get in the way of the bead when you push it back over the rim.

4 Push the valve inwards away from the rim as you begin to push the bead of the tyre over the rim. Try not to trap the tube near the valve – easily done, since this is the bulkiest section of the tube. Work around the tyre pushing the bead back over the rim with your thumbs.

5 As you get to the last section of bead to be pushed back over the rim, things can get difficult. Make sure as much of the bead as possible is pushed into the well in the middle of the rim so that you are left with the maximum amount of slack at the tight section. Do not use the tyre levers to lever the last part back on to the rim! This will pinch the tube and puncture it again. Push hard with

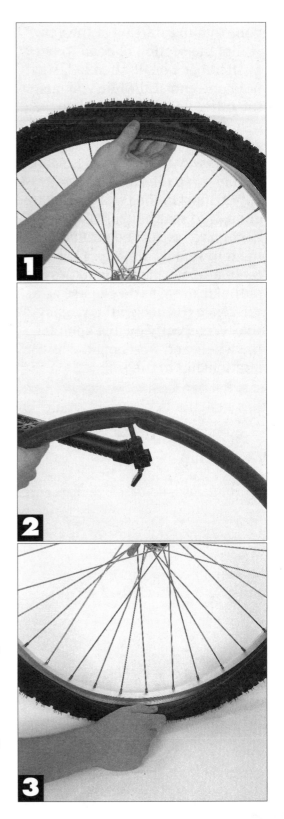

your thumbs starting at the very end of the section of bead to be pushed back on. It often helps to hold one end still while you push the other end on, rather than trying to do both at once.

6 Inflate the tyre, checking along the way that the tyre is seated evenly on to the rim. Once you get about 10psi in the tyre, it is inflated enough to seat but is still soft enough to be pushed around by hand to seat it properly. There is often a small ridge around the top of the bead that you can use as a reference to check if the tyre is seated correctly by just spinning the wheel and watching the line in relationship to the rim.

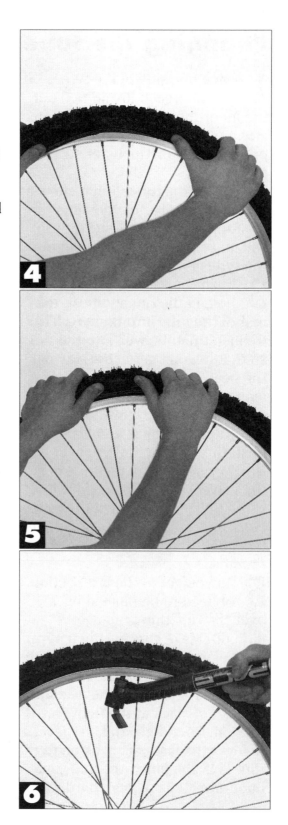

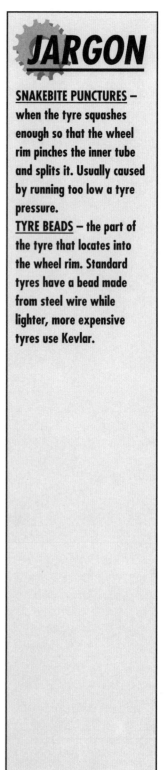

SNAKEBITE PUNCTURES – when the tyre squashes enough so that the wheel rim pinches the inner tube and splits it. Usually caused by running too low a tyre pressure.

TYRE BEADS – the part of the tyre that locates into the wheel rim. Standard tyres have a bead made from steel wire while lighter, more expensive tyres use Kevlar.

Hints 'n' tips

Tubes

Don't buy fat tubes, go for 1.5-1.75in tubes. These will fill even the huge 2.5in tyres but are much easier to get on and off because of their smaller size when partially inflated. They weigh less too, and rotating mass (wheels) is the place to save weight.

Rim tape

For ease of use and value for money, a roll of electrical tape is the cheapest and lightest rim tape. It also stays where you put it and doesn't squirm around when you are fitting or removing tyres.

Racing

For the racing edge use gas cartridges to inflate the tyre. They are much quicker than a pump and can save a lot of time. Make sure that the tyre isn't going to pop off the rim though, because they inflate the tyre quite quickly.

What to carry

If you're going somewhere far from home, it is wise to carry at least two spare tubes, a pump, and a puncture kit capable of fixing at least ten punctures. For the two-hour-blast type of ride just one tube and a trimmed down puncture kit is all that's needed. An old toe strap can be used to lash a spare tube under the seat or on to the bottom of the seat tube near the bottom bracket and down tube, below the front mech.

Pump choice

A long stroke pump will inflate a tyre faster than a short stroke one if they are the same diameter. A smaller diameter pump will take longer than a larger diameter one but will be easier to operate if high pressures are desired.

Gaffer tape

A small strip of gaffer tape (really strong sticky tape) kept around the seat tube is handy for fixing tears or cuts in the side wall of a tyre.

Knots

If you do manage to puncture without a puncture kit or spare tube with you, then tie a knot in the inner tube, leaving the hole within the knotted section. Partially inflate the tube so that the knot self tightens, then fit it back into the tyre and ride home – inflating the tube again every ten minutes or so.

THE DRIVE CHAIN

Introduction

A chain may not be the ideal way of transmitting force from the cranks to the rear wheel, but it's just about the only working method that is simple, cheap, lightweight, strong, and easy to service. Once a chain gets worn, however, the life of the sprockets driven by that chain will be drastically reduced.

When a chain wears, the distance between the rollers that contact the teeth on the sprockets becomes greater. So instead of distributing the load over four or five teeth, it all goes on to the small contact patch between just one roller and a tooth. The rollers then begin to wear at an accelerated rate. So, in the long run, it pays to look after your chain and replace it as soon as signs of wear are visible.

Looking for wear in a chain can be difficult if you don't know what to look for, but there is one method we can use that only requires a good quality ruler. Measure the length of 12 full links (the distance between 25 pins). This distance should be 12in. A chain should be replaced when the 12 link length reaches 12.125in (an eighth of an inch longer).

Replacement chains can be had from any good bike shop, but don't just buy a straight replacement. Shimano chains are widely available, but they do require special pins to join them, and this has led many people to switch to Sedis chains – the Sedis SL 8-speed chain being probably the best chain currently available for under £20. Not only does it not require special pins, it's the obvious choice for Shimano's new Compact drive 7- and 8-speed gear systems.

The Drive Chain

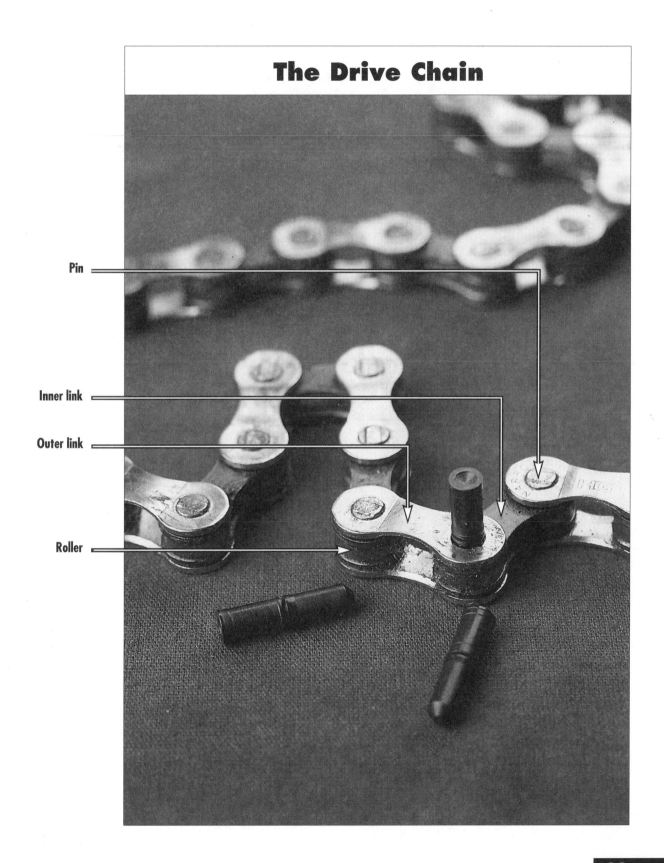

Pin

Inner link

Outer link

Roller

Cleaning with solvent

1 Wipe the chain down with a cloth soaked in cleaning solvent (buy an environmentally-friendly one if at all possible) to get the worst of the dirt off. Then, taking care not to spray solvent on to the wheel rim, hub, or bottom bracket, spray the chain and leave it for about five minutes.

2 Lightly spray the chain again and scrub out all of the links with an old brush – toothbrushes are ideal. If you use a water-soluble solvent a good blast from a hose will shift a lot of the dirt. Expect to repeat steps 1 and 2 again for a really mucky chain.

3 Wipe the chain with a clean dry rag. Hold the rag and then pedal backwards, taking care not to pull the chain to the side

JARGON

BRAKES – the system that slows/stops the bike. Usually when you pull a handlebar mounted lever. These must be kept in 100 per cent tip-top condition for the bike to be safe to ride.

CHAIN – the transmission chain that runs from the cassette to the chainset.

CHAINSET – term used to describe the front chainrings and crank arm assembly, that spins on the bottom bracket.

CRANK ARMS – the arms that come out from the bottom bracket and which carry the pedals.

DERAILLEUR – the mechanism that pushes the chain from one sprocket to the next. The front derailleur shifts the chain on the front chainrings and the rear derailleur shifts the chain on the rear gear sprockets.

FRONT MECH – the front derailleur.

LUBE/LUBRICANT, wet and dry – wet lubes stay wet to the touch when applied. Dry lubes evaporate to leave a dry film (usually teflon based). Wet lubes are good for wet conditions, while dry lubes are good for dusty conditions because they don't attract dirt.

<u>REAR MECH</u> – see derailleur Sprockets – a term used to describe the toothed sprockets of the rear gear cluster.

<u>TEFLON</u> – (see also lubes) high pressure lubricant developed by Du Pont™.

because this will bend the rear mech. Leave the chain to dry for a while in the sun – if there is any.

4 With a spray lube just hold the can near the chain and pedal backwards. Don't over do it with the lube – too much lube only attracts dirt. With bottled lubes put one drop on each roller, a dot of Tipp-ex or similar is handy for marking the start roller. Don't spin the cranks afterwards, leave the lube to soak into the chain for at least five minutes.

Cleaning with a chain cleaner

1 Wipe the chain with a solvent-soaked rag to remove the surface dirt. Then simply fill the chain cleaner with the recommended amount of solvent (usually enough to cover the bottom of the brushes), clamp it around the chain and pedal backwards. Chain cleaners really do seem to clean the chain better than any other method and are a worthwhile long-term investment.

2 Give the chain a final clean out with either fresh solvent or water if the solvent is water soluble. Leave it to dry out for a while before step 3.

3 Lube the chain, but don't over do it – too much lube only attracts dirt. Don't spin the cranks afterwards, leave the lube to soak into the chain for at least five minutes.

Splitting and fitting

1 To split a chain, run it through the ridge furthest away from the threaded driver end. Screw the driver up and seat it centrally on the pin. Then firmly screw in the driver until it pushes the pin out of the other side, taking care that the driver doesn't run off the pin and start bending the chain plates. With Shimano chains, you can push the pin all of the way out because a new special pin will be required to re-join the chain afterwards. Don't split the chain on one of the special pins because this will damage the link plate.

2 With regular chains, don't push the pin all of the way out because it needs to be pushed back in again afterwards. Leave about this much sticking out. Pull the chain out through the front and rear mech, make a note of how the chain is threaded through the rear mech if you've never done this before. To get your new chain to the same length lay it beside the old one and remove any surplus links.

3 To fit the chain, thread it through the front mech first, around the rear sprocket and then drop it down through the rear mech. Do this on the smallest sprocket at the rear and don't loop the chain over the front chainring yet, the slackness you get doing it this way helps when pulling the

two ends of the chain together. On a Sedis chain, just push the pin back in with the chain tool until both ends of the pin just protrude from the link plates. With a Shimano chain you must use the special replacement pin (sold in packs of three). Don't try using the old pin because the chain will snap in a very short time. Push the pointed end of the special pin into the chain and then drive it in with the chain tool until the end is just sticking out from the link plate. Snap off the pointed end with pliers and check that the chain isn't stiff on that link.

4 If the link is stiff, flex the chain sideways in your hands or run it over the ridge on the chain tool closest to the threaded driver. Lightly press against the pin with the driver and then check the link again. Repeat until the link rotates freely.

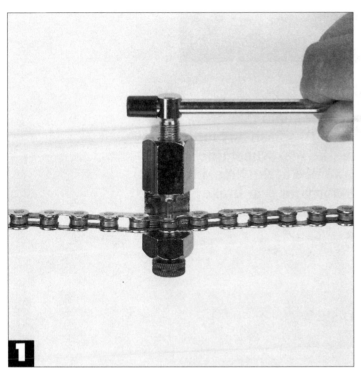

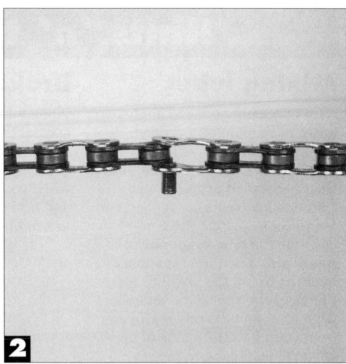

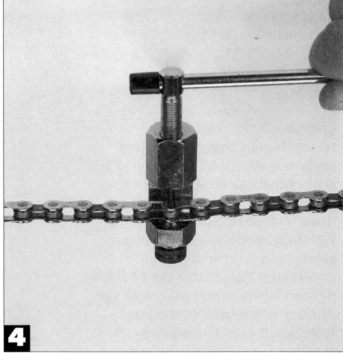

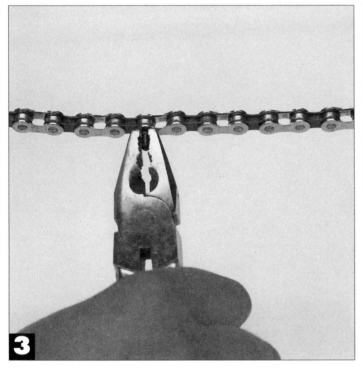

Hints 'n' tips

Mixing lubes

A lot of people prefer to apply two lubes to a chain, especially professional team mechanics. First the chain is cleaned and left to dry, then a so-called dry lubricant (often teflon based) is applied and left to soak in while the solvent carrying the lube evaporates. Afterwards a wet lube is applied over the top of the previous lube. The dry lube sits inside the rollers while the wet lube prevents water from getting to the inside of the chain. Finish Line produce two excellent lubes designed to be used this way, their dry Teflon Bicycle lube and the wet Century lube.

Lubes

Choose a lube to suit your requirements. Some lubes need replacing after every ride but don't attract too much dirt. Other lubes can stay on the chain for at least three or four rides but the chain will then need a good cleaning – it seems to attract more dirt and it stays there longer. If in doubt it's better to clean and lube the chain as often is you can. In the long term it will save you money.

Brakes

When lubing your chain take special care not to splash any lube or cleaner on the rear wheel rim. You may not notice at the time, but when you go for your rear brake and nothing happens you could be in trouble.

USING WET AND DRY LUBES
The dry lube (below) sits inside the rollers while the wet (above) lube prevents water from getting to the inside of the chain.

THE FRONT MECH
OR FRONT DERAILLEUR

Introduction

The modern front mech is a careful balance of high strength and low weight. The cage has to be strong enough to push the chain from chainring to chainring. The clamp has to be tight enough not to slip around the seat tube but, because frame tubes are getting thinner and thinner every year, it must also be designed so that it won't crush the seat tube. On top of this, there has to be some form of return spring that is strong enough to pull the chain off the large chainring to a smaller one, yet light enough so the user can push against it when shifting to a bigger one.

All of this is squeezed into a few bits of alloy, a couple of pivots and a funny shaped steel cage. The job of a front mech is a simple one, but the front mech itself is more complicated than first meets the eye, and a few millimetres of adjustment here and there can make all the difference to its performance.

The two jobs you are most likely to tackle on a front mech are changing the cable and adjusting the mech. When you change a cable make sure that the outer cables are clean and have fresh lube squirted down them, wipe lube on the new inner cable before you push it through the outers, and make sure the cable stops are cleaned out prior to installation.

The Front Derailleur

Cable end cap

Frame clamp bolt

Little ring adjusting screw

Big ring adjusting screw

Cable clamp bolt

Outer cage plate

Inner cage plate

Replacing a cable

1 Set the gear shifter to the inner chainring position and undo the cable clamp bolt on the front mech. Pull the inner cable from the outers as you remove the outers from the frame (make note of what piece of outer went where on the frame and any guides or pulleys the inner went through). Remove the cable cover from the rear of the shifter (if fitted) and push the cable until the nipple pops out. Pull the cable all of the way out of the shifter.

2 Clean out the cable outers and spray them with light lube. Push the new cable through the shifter and replace any cable covers on the shifter. Thread the inner cable through the outers and replace them in their stops on the frame. Screw the barrel adjuster on the shifter all of the way in (clockwise) and then two full turns back out. Thread the inner cable through any guides or pulleys and then under the clamp bolt on the front mech. Pull the cable tight with either some pliers or a third hand tool and tighten the clamp bolt.

3 Trim the cable to length (leave about an inch) and fit a cable end cap. This makes the job look neat and tidy and also stops the cable fraying – frayed cables can catch on your calves.

JARGON

CABLES – the wire system used to operate brakes and gears. Consisting of an inner section which is pulled (tension), and an outer section which is squeezed (compressed). Both inner and outer must be in good condition to operate under tension and compression.

CHAIN – the transmission chain that runs from the cassette to the chainset.

DEGREASER – solvent which will remove grease. Useful for cleaning components, especially the chain when used with a chain cleaning tool.

GRIPSHIFT – a gear shifting system in which a section of the handlebar grip rotates.

INDEXED FRONT MECH/GEARS – in the past you had to try to select a gear by 'feeling' the tension in the gearshift handle and cable. Now each gear has its own slot and when you change gear there you decide which one you want (assuming it's all adjusted properly).There's usually a click-stop thumb shifter or two independent levers, one for shifting up and one for shifting down. The

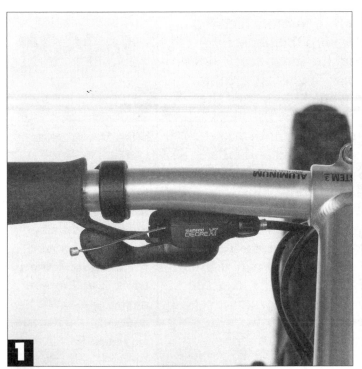

Adjustment

1 To work properly the front mech outer cage plate should be 1-2mm above the big chainring. To adjust the height of the mech, undo (anti-clockwise) the clamp bolt on the main clamp that goes around the frame tube. The bolt will either be on the lefthand side of the bike for a 'hinge' type clamp or on the righthand side of the mech alloy body for the 'endless band' type. If your chainrings aren't round then set the mech 1-2mm from the highest part of the ring.

2 The outer cage plate must be set parallel to the chainrings. Look down from above as you twist the mech on the frame tube, but be careful not to move the mech up or down because this will affect any adjustment you made in step 1. Some mechs move as you tighten the clamp bolt and this movement will have to be taken into account if the mech is to be correctly aligned when the bolt is tightened. A clamp bolt doesn't have to be mega tight, especially on thin-walled frame tubes. Tighten it just enough so that you can't move the mech when you try and rotate it with both hands. The only thing trying to move the front mech is cable tension, aside from that there is no other reason for the mech to move.

3 The limit screws adjust the point where the mech is physically stopped from moving.

The outer screw controls the stop when shifting into the largest chainring and the inner screw does the inner chainring. If, after cable installation, you can't engage the large chainring, screw the limit screw anti-clockwise until you can. If the chain over-shifts and falls over the chainring on to the crank, screw the limit screw clock-wise until it stops over-shifting.

If you can't engage the small chainring, screw the limit screw anti-clockwise until you can. If the chain over-shifts and falls over the chainring into the bottom bracket area, screw the limit screw clockwise until it stops over-shifting. If the limit screw is screwed all of the way out and you still can't engage the small chainring check that there isn't too much cable tension by turning the barrel adjuster on the shifter clockwise to decrease cable tension. You usually have to ride backwards and forwards carrying a screwdriver and re-adjusting until things are sorted. It can be done on a bike stand, but you'll usually find that the front mech shifts differently when under power.

4 To adjust an indexed front mech, shift into the middle ring and turn the barrel adjuster until the chain doesn't rub on the mech plates in any of the rear gears. Turn the adjuster clockwise to bring the cage closer to the frame, and anti-clockwise to bring it closer to the outer chainring.

JARGON

advantage is quick and precise gear changes
LUBE/LUBRICANT, WET AND DRY – wet lubes stay wet to the touch when applied. Dry lubes evaporate to leave a dry film (usually teflon based). Wet lubes are good for wet conditions, while dry lubes are good for dusty conditions because they don't attract dirt
RAPID FIRE – Shimano gear lever system consisting of a thumb-operated lever behind and underneath the handlebar for shifting down the gears and a finger operated lever in front of the bar for shifting up the gears
SEAT TUBE – the part of the frame that the seat post fits into
TEFLON – (see also lubes) high pressure lubricant developed by Du Pont™
Thumbshifters – gear shifting levers mounted above the handlebar operated by the thumbs.

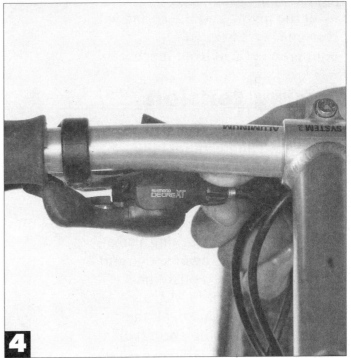

Hints 'n' tips

Mech removal

When removing a front mech it is not necessary to split the chain. Unscrew the small cross head screw that holds the two mech cage plates together, at the rear end of the cage, then pull them apart gently until the chain can be removed from within the cage.

Mech cleaning and lubing

A dousing with degreaser, a scrubbing with a small brush, and a good application of light lube to all of the pivots and the spring will restore even the most temperamental of front mechs.

Spring tension

On front mechs designed to be used with Thumbshifters the spring tension is greater than those designed for use with Rapid Fire. On old-style Shimano DX and XT front mechs the spring tension can be adjusted by turning a small barrel that sits up against one end of the spring. If you push the spring out of the way with a screwdriver and shake out the barrel, the end of the spring will come further out than usual – and spring tension will be decreased. Removing the small black barrel will allow any old-style mech to work perfectly with the new style Rapid Fire shifters and the popular Gripshift shifters.

Spring tension adjustment

Spring tension adjuster

On older-style Shimano DX and XT front mechs, the spring tension can be adjusted by turning a small barrel that sits up against one end of the spring.

THE REAR MECH
OR REAR DERAILLEUR

Introduction

In design terms a rear mech is something of a compromise. It's a collection of simple levers and two toothed wheels held in a flimsy cage, all pivoting on a bolt through the frame. It has the job of pushing the chain from one cog to the next and does so using just cable or spring tension.

It's engineered just enough to do the job. By skimping on the depth of tooth profiles (so they wear faster) and messing around with the chain link profiles (which makes them weaker) the rest of the transmission system has been 'softened up' just enough to let a remarkably lightweight and simple rear mech do the job without breaking.

Bad shifting can often be traced to the cables and the rear derailleur alone is rarely the source of the problem. Over-shifting (where the chain is pushed past the largest sprocket into the wheel) or under-shifting (where the chain won't go on to the smallest sprocket) are easy to remedy, although if a bike starts to do this for no apparent reason there is a strong chance that the derailleur hanger (the part of the frame it screws on to) is bent, or the derailleur cage itself is bent.

Common Rear Derailleur

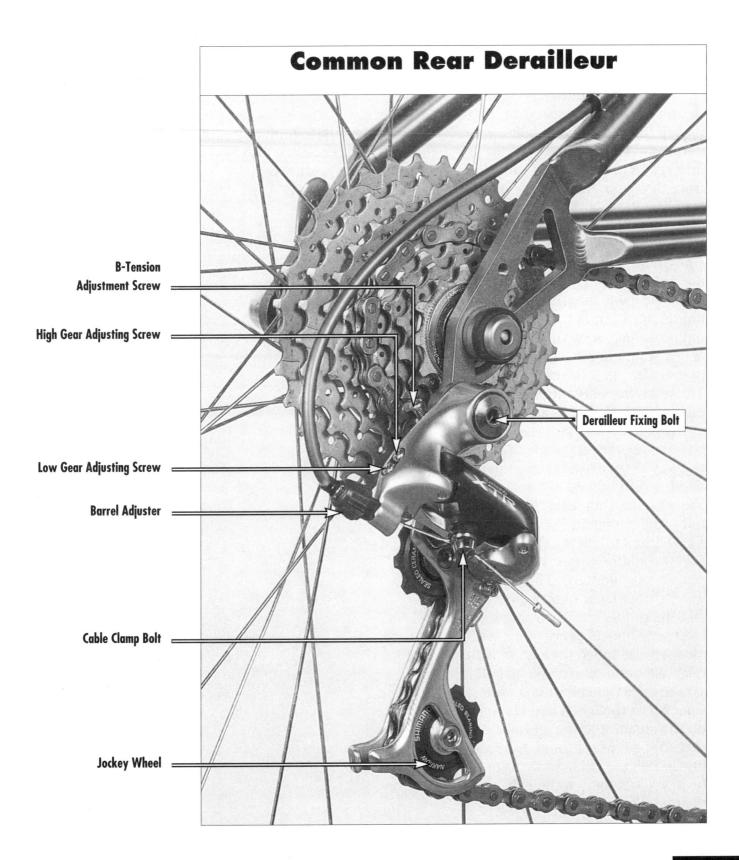

B-Tension
Adjustment Screw

High Gear Adjusting Screw

Derailleur Fixing Bolt

Low Gear Adjusting Screw

Barrel Adjuster

Cable Clamp Bolt

Jockey Wheel

Cable replacement

1 Change gear until the chain is on the smallest sprocket, then loosen the cable clamp bolt on the derailleur. Remove the end cap (if fitted) and pull the inner cable from the outer. Remove the outers from the frame and note which piece of outer came from which part of the bike.

2 On Rapid Fire shifters, pop out the small plug-in cover and push the cable inner until the nipple pops out of the hole (some old units have a small crosshead screw which holds a cover in place), then pull the cable out. Thumbshifters are much easier – just push the cable, grab the nipple and pull out the cable. Screw the barrel adjuster on the mech all of the way in (clockwise) and then one full turn out again. Do the same on the shifter but with two full turns out again.

3 Thread the new cable through the shifter and replace the plug-in cap (if fitted). Thread the inner through the outers and then slot the outers into their stops on the frame, making sure you have cleaned and lubed the outers with degreaser and lube or WD40 before you re-insert the new inner wire. Check that the mech and chain are on the smallest sprocket then thread the inner through the rear mech. Pull the cable until there is no slack and tighten the cable clamp bolt. Trim the inner sticking out of the clamp bolt, leaving about an inch, and fit a new end cap.

4 Unscrew (anti-clockwise) the barrel adjuster until any cable slack is removed. Then move on to the 'adjusting' section on page 52.

CABLES – the wire system used to operate brakes and gears. Consisting of an inner section which is pulled (tension), and an outer section which is squeezed (compressed). Both inner and outer must be in good condition to operate under tension and compression.
DERAILLEUR – the mechanism that pushes the chain from one sprocket to the next. The front derailleur shifts the chain on the front chainrings and the rear derailleur shifts the chain on the rear gear sprockets.
INDEXED GEARS – in the past you had to try to select a gear by 'feeling' the tension in the gearshift handle and cable. Now each gear has its own slot and when you change gear there you decide which one you want (assuming it's all adjusted properly).There's usually a click-stop thumb shifter or two independent levers, one for shifting up and one for shifting down. The advantage is quick and precise gear changes.

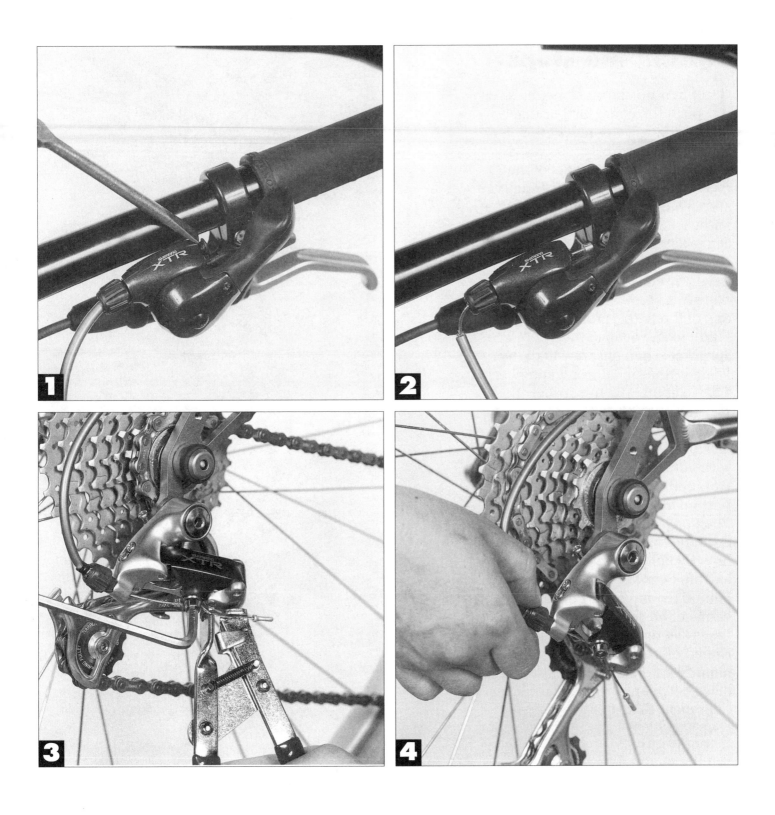

Setting the stops

1 A rear mech can sometimes push the chain further than necessary, and to prevent this there are two screw stops which physically limit the travel of the mech. To set the smallest sprocket stop, shift into the smallest sprocket (it's better to do this job at the same time as changing the cable, then cable tension doesn't have any effect) and screw in the adjusting screw – usually the top one of the two – until the chain starts to rub against the second sprocket. Then unscrew until the chain misses the second sprocket.

2 To adjust the top sprocket stop, shift into the largest sprocket (without the cable you can just push the mech across with your hand) and screw in the stop until the chain starts to get pushed off the largest sprocket. Then unscrew the stop slightly until the top jockey wheel is directly below the sprocket. When a chain over-shifts it can drop behind the largest sprocket and damage the spokes, or in severe cases the rear mech can even be ripped off the frame. Some bike manufacturers fit small plastic discs between wheel and sprocket to prevent this.

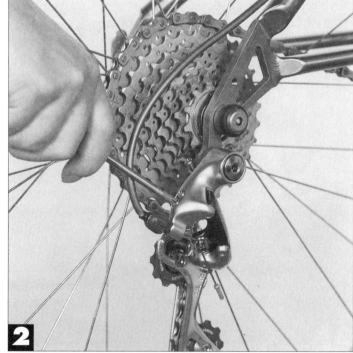

Adjustment and indexing

1 Indexed gear systems from Shimano and Suntour differ in the way they are set up. Suntour are better adjusted for shifting from smallest to the second sprocket, while Shimano are better set up for shifting from the second to third sprocket. Indexing adjustments are made by increasing or decreasing the cable tension using the barrel adjusters.

2 With a Shimano system, shift into the second sprocket (increase cable tension with the adjusters until you can shift from smallest to the second sprocket first of all) and screw the adjuster out until the chain just begins to rub on the third sprocket. Screw the adjuster back in a quarter of a turn and try the shifting. If the chain hesitates when shifting to a larger sprocket you need more cable tension and the barrel adjuster will have to be turned anti-clockwise. If it hesitates when dropping to a smaller cog, it means less tension is required and the adjuster should be turned clockwise. Adjust a small amount at a time and try the shifting between each adjustment. For Suntour the procedure is the same except you begin with the chain on the smallest sprocket.

Hints 'n' tips

Cable care

The simplest way to clean and lubricate gear cables is to shift into the largest sprocket and then shift into the smallest sprocket without pedalling or turning the wheel. This will create a lot of slack in the cable so the outer cables can be pulled out of the stops on the frame. Slide the outers along to expose the normally covered inner section and wipe them with a clean cloth soaked in thin lube.

Mech cleaning

Blasting the rear mech with water is fine, so long as you don't blast the jockey wheels. A squirt of WD40 afterwards will repel the water and a generous application of thick lube in all of the pivots and on the spring will keep things running smoothly until the next hosing down.

B tension

The B tension screw (the small cross head screw that butts up against the rear of the mech hanger on the frame) adjusts the distance from the top jockey pulley to the sprockets. If it's too close, shifting to a larger sprocket will be difficult; if too far away, shifting to smaller sprockets will often result

in shifting two gears instead of one. Screwing the adjuster in (clockwise) pushes the pulley away from the sprockets, screwing it out brings the pulley closer to the sprockets.

Jockey wheels

Worn jockey wheels don't push the chain as efficiently, so your shifting suffers. Shimano's top jockey wheel floats slightly from side to side, so make sure you get the correct 'Centeron G Pulley' replacement.

Damaged cables

The wire strands or outer gear cables run along the length of the cable and are not wound around spirally as in brake cables. When the hard plastic outer becomes weak the inner wires can expand under compression and the gear shifting becomes spongy and imprecise. New outers with correctly installed end caps must be fitted to restore shifting performance.

JARGON

JOCKEY WHEEL – the two small wheels in the rear derailleur.

RAPID FIRE – Shimano gear lever system consisting of a thumb-operated lever behind and underneath the handlebar for shifting down the gears and a finger operated lever in front of the bar for shifting up the gears.

SPROCKETS – a term used to describe the toothed sprockets of the rear gear cluster.

THUMBSHIFTERS – gear shifting levers mounted above the handlebar operated by the thumbs.

WD-40 – a penetrating oil used for freeing jammed fasteners, seat posts, stems, and so on. It is also very good at dispersing water – handy after you've washed the bike and you want to blast the water out of sensitive parts like the chain and gear/brake cables.

Slotted cable stops allow for easy cable care.

BRAKES

Introduction

The brakes are one of the most important components on a bike. I cannot stress too much how important it is to look after your braking system – your life may depend on it. Inspect your cables regularly, preferably before every ride, and check for brake block or pad wear at least once every two weeks.

Brakes

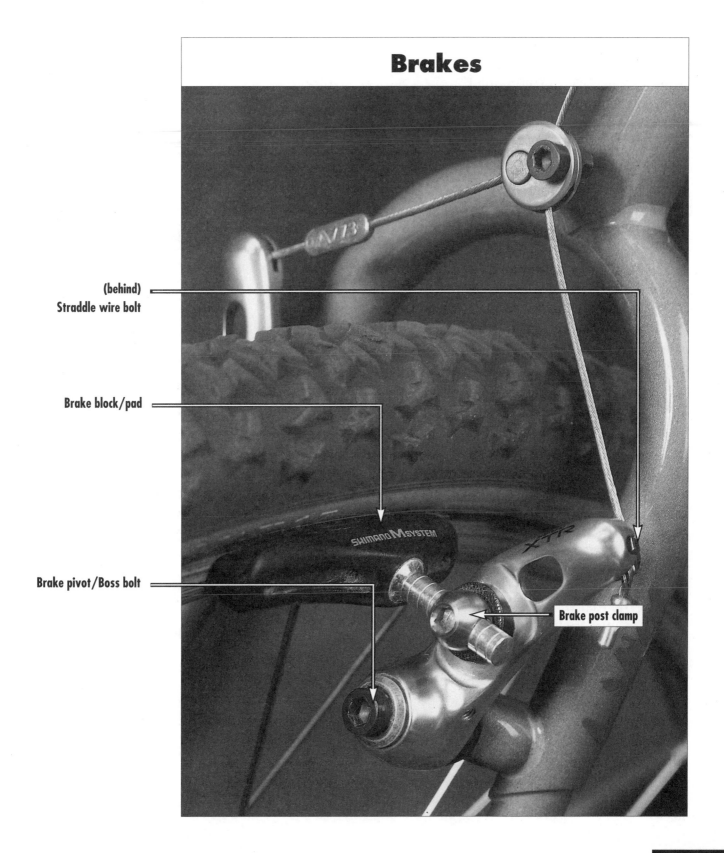

(behind)
Straddle wire bolt

Brake block/pad

Brake pivot/Boss bolt

Brake post clamp

1 (The tyre has been removed to make the steps easier to see.) Remove the straddle wire quick release as if you were going to remove the wheel. Undo the cable clamp from the other brake arm and disconnect the cable. Next, unscrew (anti-clockwise) the brake boss bolts (5mm Allen key)

2 Clean the brake bosses and the inside of the brake bush that fits over the boss. Re-install the brake on the boss and check that it rotates freely with no tight spots. Paint over-spray can be removed with fine emery paper sprayed with WD40 or similar. Grease the boss thoroughly after cleaning but don't get grease down the threads that run inside it.

3 Clean out the springs (run a rag between each coil) and then grease them to prevent corrosion. Do one cantilever at a time so as not to get the springs mixed up. If you do mix them up, then the wire of the spring should wind outwards and away from the wheel – opposite to that shown in the picture. The spring locates in a hole at the rear of the boss and, usually, there are three holes to choose from which allows you to adjust the spring tension. However, the middle hole is the best place to start.

4 Re-install the brake making sure that the spring engages in the recess inside the rear of the brake. Tighten the boss bolts tightly, but don't go over the top

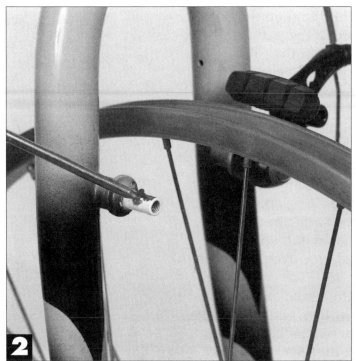

2

3

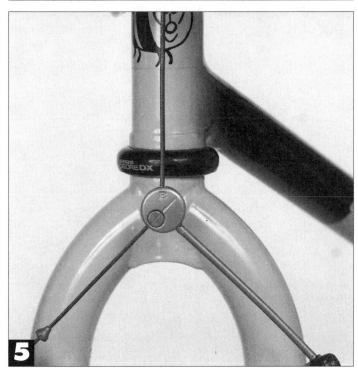

5

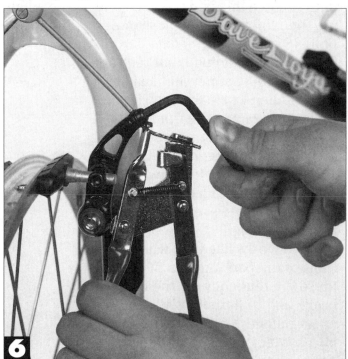

6

because it is easy to deform the boss and that will make the brake bind. Use a drop of thread-locking compound on all bolts connected with the braking system.

5 This shows by far the most common straddle wire system. The main brake cable runs through the lefthand side of the yoke and through the small diameter inner to the lefthand cantilever. A short link wire runs from the yoke to the righthand cantilever and has a small line marked on it. When this marking is in line with the marking on the yoke it is correctly set up.

6 Thread the cables into place and pull the main cable through on the lefthand cantilever until the two lines on the yoke line up, then tighten the cable clamp bolt.

7 Brake pad adjustment requires a 10mm spanner and, usually, a 5mm Allen key – although some brakes use 6mm. The front of the block should be 2mm away from the rim, and the rear of the pad should be 3mm to 4mm away. This arrangement is called 'toe-in' alignment and prevents the brakes from squealing.

Toe-in works like this: when the front of the pad touches the rim there is a tendency for the whole brake unit to flex slightly, which in effect pulls the rest of the block into contact with the rim (it happens anyway when you pull hard on the brake lever). If the front of the brake pad was further away from the rim than the back, then the front of the pad would be pushed away from the rim and the brake would vibrate and squeal.

8 The new style of brake uses a cross head screw to adjust the spring tension. Tightening the screw increases the spring tension on the cantilever and pushes it away from the rim, loosening brings it closer. A few pulls of the brake between adjustments and each pad should end up exactly the same distance from the wheel rim.

9 Finish the brake cable off neatly with an end cap. Leave about one to two inches of cable sticking out, then tuck it behind the small pin on the back of the brake so it's out of the way.

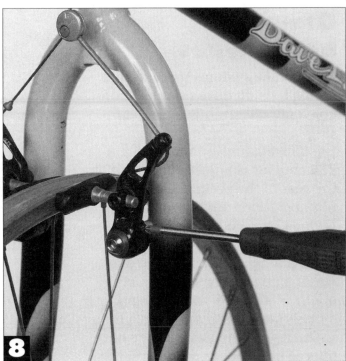

Other brake types

Some brake systems use different spring tension devices and a more conventional straddle wire set up.

A Spring tension on some brakes is adjusted by a nut at the rear of the brake. Loosen the boss bolt and turn the nut (usually with a 13mm cone spanner – Dia-Compe) until the desired tension is achieved. Some brakes have one either side and some have just the one side with the other being the more conventional spring in a hole at the rear of the boss. If they have nuts at both sides you must set both sides to the desired tension and then adjust one of them until they are balanced.

B A hanger and straddle wire like this used to be the most common system until Shimano stopped using it, but that doesn't mean it's no good – in fact many still argue that it is better. Most brakes work better if the angle between the straddle wire and the cantilever (a line taken through the boss and where the cable attaches) is close to 90° (see diagram) when the pads touch the wheel rim. A hanger set up like this is very easy to adjust and you can easily experiment with cable angles – hence it's popularity.

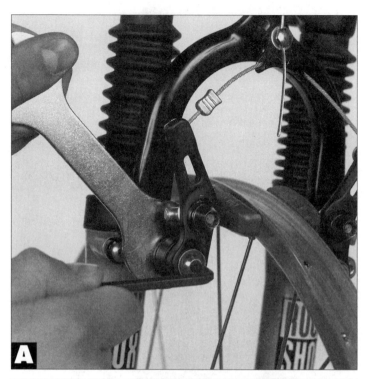

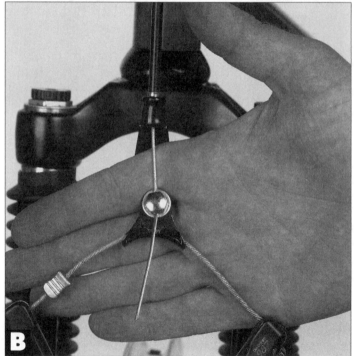

Hints 'n' tips

BRAKE BLOCKS – the rubber pads that locate into the brake and press against the wheel rim when you pull the brake lever.

CABLES – the wire system used to operate brakes and gears. Consisting of an inner section which is pulled (tension), and an outer section which is squeezed (compressed). Both inner and outer must be in good condition to operate under tension and compression.

QUICK RELEASE/QR – a lever mechanism for fastening the wheel quickly and easily into the frame/forks. The QR runs through the wheel axle, and when the lever is closed it applies force between its ends in much the same way as tightening wheel nuts.

WD-40 – a penetrating oil used for freeing jammed fasteners, seat posts, stems, and so on. It is also very good at dispersing water – handy after you've washed the bike and you want to blast the water out of sensitive parts like the chain and gear/brake cables.

Brake blocks or pads

As the brake pads wear, their contact point with the rim moves downwards (U-brakes are the opposite and the pads tend to move up and touch the tyre), and the cantilever has to swing further towards the rim, which requires more lever travel. It is important to keep a check on the wear, because badly worn pads can get pushed under the wheel rim and jam in the spokes.

Custom pad work

Pads that have a lip worn into them can be re-used simply by cutting the lip off with a sharp knife and then re-flatting the pad with a file. Often with shallow-walled wheel rims the ends of some long brake pads nearly rub on the tyre while the middle of the pad doesn't fit on to the rim properly. Shape the end edges of the pad with a sharp knife until the middle seats perfectly on the rim and the ends miss the tyre.

Cables

Also high on the danger list are the brake cables. A snapped brake cable means either no brake power

Frayed cables mean dangerous cables; anything in this state must be replaced – immediately.

at all or, if the straddle wire drops on to the tyre and locks the wheel, total braking at an unexpected moment. Either way a recipe for disaster. Check all cables regularly, especially in any places where they are clamped and at the nipple end.

THE CHAINSET
AND BOTTOM BRACKET

Introduction

The chainset and bottom bracket are at the heart of the transmission system and can be the source of major problems, as well as those annoying little squeaks and creaks that take ages to find.

   Start by cleaning the bike thoroughly, this makes the job much more pleasant right from the start...

The Chainset and Bottom Bracket

Chainset

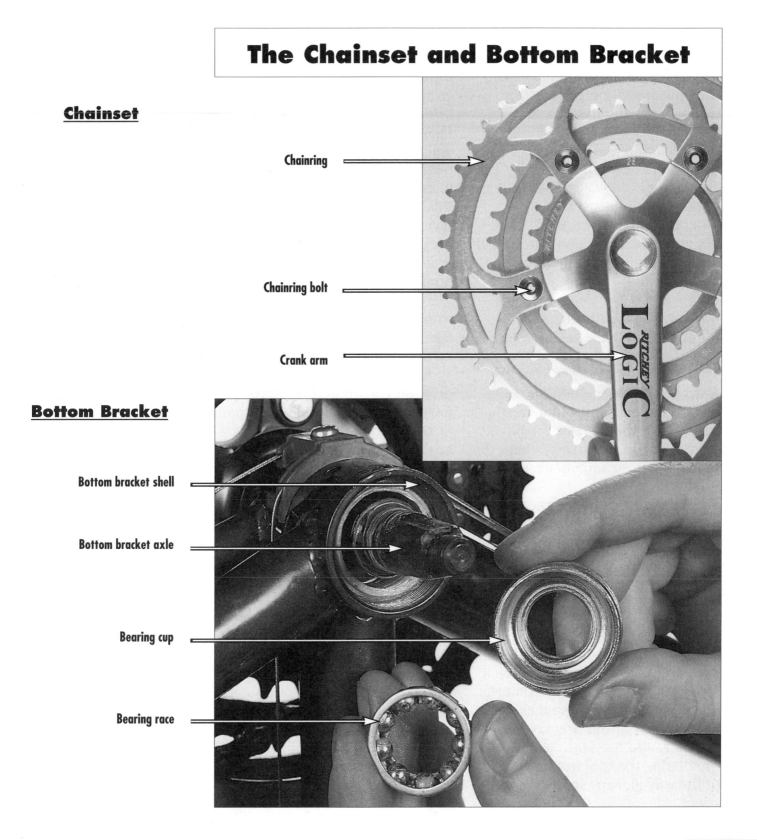

Chainring

Chainring bolt

Crank arm

Bottom Bracket

Bottom bracket shell

Bottom bracket axle

Bearing cup

Bearing race

Fitting

1 The first step is to remove the crank arms, complete with chainrings, from the bottom bracket. Remove any dust caps that are fitted and then unscrew the crank bolts anti-clockwise. The crank bolts will vary depending upon what cranks you have. Modern Shimano are 8mm Allen key, older stuff are 14mm hex head bolt (the socket found on the end of most crank extractors), Campagnolo use 15mm hex headed bolts and some aftermarket American units are half-inch Imperial hex-headed bolts. Titanium bolts vary from 6mm Allen key (Royce), 8mm Allen key, or 12mm,13mm and 14mm hex head. Once they've been removed have a look in the recess where the bolt came from and check for any washers.

2 Screw the crank extractor into the large thread inside the recess of the crank arm. Be careful at first because it is easy to damage this thread if you have not aligned the extractor correctly. It's wise to clean the threads out first with a blast of WD 40 or similar.

Screw the extractor all of the way in until it stops (don't force it once it stops), then check that the driver tool head that pushes against the bottom bracket axle isn't screwed too far in and is preventing the tool from going all of the way in. Now screw the central part of the extractor in until it touches the axle, then keep turning it with a spanner until the crank arm is pulled off the bottom bracket axle. If the crank has never been removed it may be quite tight and a blast of penetrating oil in between the crank and the axle is highly recommended. If you do this, wait a few minutes before trying again. If things still won't budge then pour hot water over that part of the crank while gently tapping the central part of the extractor with a rubber hammer or wooden mallet.

3 Recent Shimano cartridge bottom brackets require special tool TL-UN52. The non drive side of all bottom brackets unscrew anti-clockwise (righthand thread), while the drive side unscrews clockwise (lefthand thread). More traditional bottom brackets have lockrings fitted which must be unscrewed first (same threads as above) with a regular bottom bracket tool. Once the lockring is off unscrew the cup from the frame with a peg spanner (usually on the other end of the bottom bracket tool). For Shimano cartridge units, just unscrew the non-drive side cup and then the drive side cup (the whole unit comes out with this side). All of this is usually quite tight so don't be afraid to be firm.

4 When replacing a bottom bracket, take the whole lot to the bike shop in the order it came

JARGON

ALLEN KEY – hexagonal-shaped rod bent at 90° that fits into the head of an Allen bolt. Almost every bike uses Allen bolts

BOTTOM BRACKET – the bearing and axle assembly in the frame which the crank assembly fastens to.

CARTRIDGE – a type of bearing. The outer race, balls, and inner race are one assembly. The whole cartridge must be replaced when it becomes worn.

CHAINSET – term used to describe the front chainrings and crank arm assembly, that spins on the bottom bracket.

CRANK ARMS – the arms that come out from the bottom bracket and which carry the pedals.

DEGREASER – solvent which will remove grease. Useful for cleaning components, especially the chain when used with a chain cleaning tool.

GEAR PULLER – automotive tool used for removing gears. Can be useful on mountain bikes for removing stubborn or damaged crank arms.

off the bike. Take note of any markings that indicate which way round things should be fitted. With conventional loose-ball bottom brackets, clean everything thoroughly, inspect the axle and cup bearing surfaces for wear, and replace the ball bearings. If the cups or axle surfaces are worn it's wise to replace the whole unit rather than try and purchase individual parts.

5 **a)** Thoroughly clean and grease the threads in the bottom bracket shell before re-installing the bottom bracket. **b)** Begin re-assembly from the drive side. With older loose-ball bottom brackets, screw the fixed cup (the one with the two flats on it) very tightly into the frame. On modern Shimano units, screw the whole unit into the frame tightly until the lip butts up against the bottom bracket shell, then screw the other cup into the non-drive side until it stops tight. With loose-ball units, screw the adjustable cup in until you feel the bearings begin to bind slightly, then screw the lockring up to the frame. Tighten the lockring while holding the cup firmly in position. Tightening the lockring should pull the cup outwards just enough to remove the slight binding of the bearings. If not, loosen the lockring, slacken the cup slightly, and then re-tighten the lockring. Repeat the procedure until the axle turns smoothly and there is no play in the bearings.

6 Make sure that the tapers of the bottom bracket shell and inside the crank arms are clean and dry. Use a degreaser on them and then wipe them dry with a clean dry cloth. Leave them for a while until they have dried off properly. Do this step now, then when you've done the chainring sections coming up next they will be clean and dry ready for the cranks to be re-fitted.

7 If the chainrings are in good condition, check that all of the chainring bolts are tight (clockwise). You'll need a wide-bladed screwdriver or Shimano tool TL-FC20 for the nut part at the rear, and a 5mm Allen key for the bolt part. To remove the chainrings unscrew all of the bolts, starting with the smallest chainring first. Make a note of any spacers that are present and where exactly they were fitted.

8 Grease the chainring bolts before re-assembly, but take care not to get grease on the outside of the nut part because this will cause it to slip inside the recess on the chainring.

9 Grease the crank bolts after pushing the crank arms on to their tapers. Tighten them firmly with a regular length Allen key (max torque is 22ftlbs). After a few hours riding, tighten them again and check them at regular intervals. Once the cranks settle on to the axle they shouldn't come loose.

LOCKRING – the small threaded ring that hold the rear gear sprockets on a freehub.
PEG SPANNER – spanner consisting of two pegs that locate into holes on the component. Commonly used for bottom bracket cups TL-UN52, TL-FC20, TL-HG15, TL-PD40 – Shimano special tool code numbers (quote the appropriate one when buying a special tool).
WD-40 – a penetrating oil used for freeing jammed fasteners, seat posts, stems, and so on. It is also very good at dispersing water – handy after you've washed the bike and you want to blast the water out of sensitive parts like the chain and gear/brake cables.

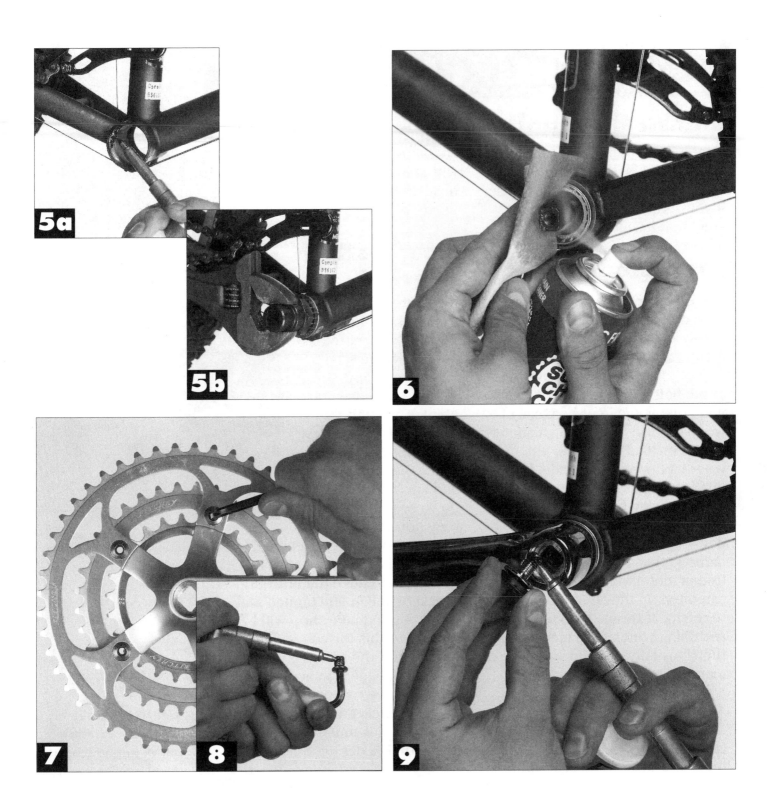

Hints 'n' tips

Lightweight bolts

Titanium or aluminium bolts should only be used once the cranks have settled on to the axle, if your cranks come loose use a steel bolt to tighten them with.

Damaged cranks

Removing cranks with damaged extractor threads can be done in several ways, but by far the best – if you have to re-use the crank, that is – is to simply remove the crank bolt and ride your bike. If you must you can use a piece of wood (a 'drift') and a big hammer on the back of the crank arm where it fits on to the axle, but this often damages the crank.

Try pouring hot water over the crank prior to this method, but never apply direct heat or a naked flame to the cranks. A gear puller from a motor vehicle tool suppliers can often do the trick. Try popping to the local garage at lunch time and asking one of the mechanics, they'll usually do it for the price of a pint or two.

Washing

Never, ever, ever jet wash the bottom bracket. The seals on bottom brackets are only just good enough to keep out the rain and water from occasional stream crossings, they won't even withstand a blast from a garden hose. Instead, use a stiff brush and plenty of hot soapy water.

New bottom bracket

If you are swapping from old cup-and-cone bottom bracket to a new cartridge type take note of any screws or grease nipples fitted to the bottom bracket. These may interfere with the fitting of the new unit and should be trimmed down or removed so they don't stick too far into the bottom bracket shell. While you have the chance it is a good idea to have the bottom bracket shell in line tapped and faced. A good bike shop will be able to do this for you and it will ensure that the bearings are perfectly aligned, thus reducing wear and the risk of failure. (Some bottom bracket axle manufacturers state that this must be done before fitting their axles).

Above: Cup-and-cone bottom bracket

Right: The bad news for lazy off-roaders is that bottom brackets are never going to be 'fit and forget' components, no matter which price range you choose from.

THE WHEEL HUBS

Introduction

Just like most bearings on a bike your wheel hubs have to support the weight of bike and rider and cope with the huge impact loads generated by off-road riding. The very nature of mountain biking means that they are probably going to be submersed in mucky water occasionally, which means they will need servicing at least twice a year – and preferably once every two or three months.

Problems with wheel bearings tend to be very simple. The wheel will either rattle from side to side (loose bearings) or it won't spin freely (tight bearings). Either fault will result in the swift self-destruction of the bearings.

The freehub or freewheel problems are usually simple too. Either the pawls inside are damaged, or they are full of gunge. The symptoms are easy to spot, the cogs will turn freely in both directions with no clicking noise, or will 'slip' from time to time. Sometimes they can be rescued by dousing them with a penetrating oil like WD40, but it's often safer to fit a new unit.

JARGON

ALLEN KEY – hexagonal-shaped rod bent at 90° that fits into the head of an Allen bolt. Almost every bike uses Allen bolts.
CASSETTE – term used to describe the cluster of gear sprockets on the rear wheel.
CHAIN WHIP – tool used to hold the rear gear sprockets while the lockring or threaded sprocket are removed.
CONE – the cone shaped part of a bearing assembly. Used with a cup and bearings.
FLANGE – the part of the hub the spokes thread through.

The Wheel Hub

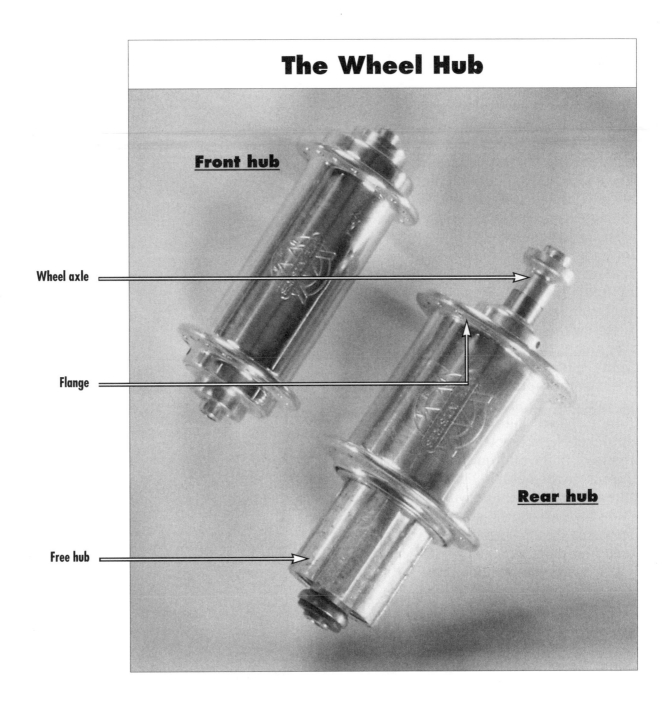

Front hub

Wheel axle

Flange

Rear hub

Free hub

Fitting

1 Remove the wheel from the bike and remove the quick release. On the back wheel you'll have to remove the gear cassette. Place a chain whip around the second largest sprocket and place Shimano tool TL-HG15 (or aftermarket equivalent) in the lockring. Next spin the quick release back through the axle and tighten it just enough to stop the tool from falling out of the lockring. Unscrew the lockring anti-clockwise (they're usually quite tight). Under this lockring there is a removable sprocket (with 11, 12 or 13 teeth), probably a washer (funny shaped), and the rest of the sprockets held together with either rivets or bolts. Suntour rear sprockets are held on by a threaded sprocket and will require two chain whips, the smallest end sprocket should then be unscrewed anti-clockwise.

2 Now the other side of the wheel – the non-drive side. First, carefully remove any rubber covers that might be fitted. On this end of the axle there is a locknut, some spacers, and the cone. Using the cone spanner (usually 15mm for rear and 13mm for front) loosen the locknut by holding the cone and turning the locknut anti-clockwise.

3 Remove the lockring and spacers, making note of their

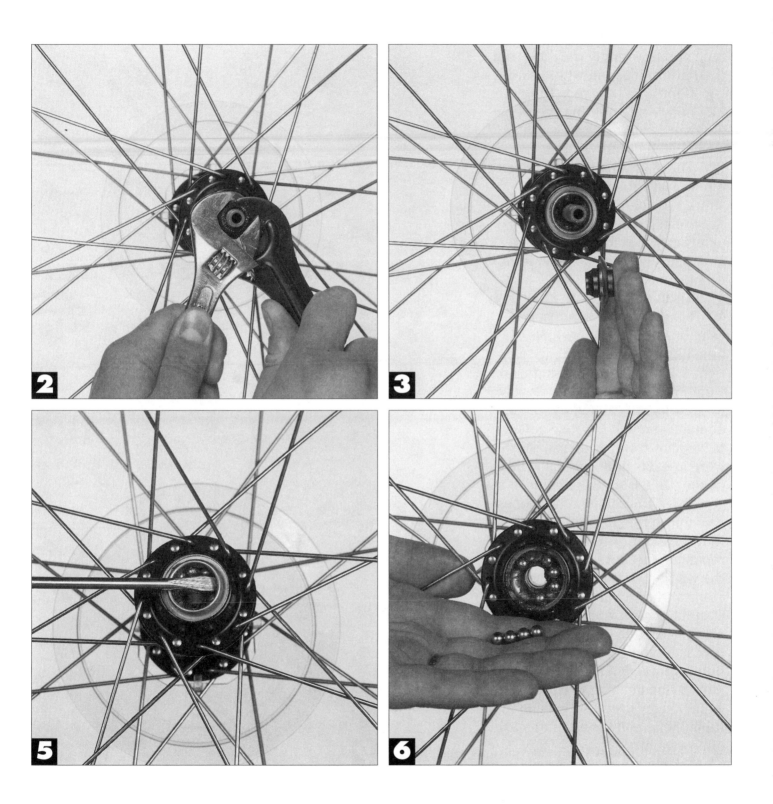

type and how many they are, and then put them somewhere safe.

4 Gently pull the axle from the hub, while holding the wheel flat over a container to catch any stray ball bearings.

5 There usually isn't any need to remove the dustcaps, but should the bearings refuse to come out the cap can be removed by using a wide-bladed screwdriver and gently working around it until it pops out.

6 Clean and check the ball bearings, cones, cups, and axle for signs of damage. Small hole like pits are a result of over-tightening and/or water ingress which causes rust. Dents or wave like marks are caused by impact damage, a result of loose cones. Make a note of how many balls were in each side, and also which cones came from which side. It's a good idea to assemble the cones back on to the axle in the order that they came off. If you need any replacement parts it's wise to take the whole axle and cone assembly, along with the ball bearings, to the shop to ensure you get the correct bits. If the cups in the hub are damaged you'll have to buy new hubs, although a lightly damaged pair of hubs can be used for a little while longer if you are willing to replace the ball bearings at least once a month.

7 Should you need to replace the freehub on the rear wheel you'll find it is held on by a hollow

bolt that requires a 10mm Allen key and unscrews anti-clockwise. The freehub itself is located on splines that protrude from the outer side of the hub flange and comes off as a whole unit. When you refit it's wise to grease the threads thoroughly and tighten the bolt very firmly with a regular length Allen key only. Do not use long Allen keys or apply any extra leverage.

8 Everything should be spotlessly clean before you get to this stage. For re-assembly put plenty of fresh grease in the cups and then seat the bearings firmly into the grease. It's a good idea to fit brand new ball bearings at every rebuild, so that any deformed bearings don't get re-installed.

9 If the dustcaps were removed they should be gently refitted. A light tap with a rubber hammer is all you'll need. Seals on most modern hubs only need to be pushed in far enough to clear the cover fitted to the cone and no further, and finger pressure alone is often enough.

10 Re-assemble the drive side cone and locknut on to the axle, replacing any spacers that were fitted between them. Screw the lock nut on until 5mm of axle is left protruding, then tighten the cone hard against the locknut. Refit any seals and push the axle through the hub until it seats against the drive side bearings.

Screw the cone on the other side along with any spacers and the locknut.

To adjust the bearings, turn the cone until you feel it bind against the bearings. Loosen it off a tiny amount until the wheel turns freely and then tighten the locknut against it. The bearings should be ever so slightly loose so that when the wheel is clamped in the frame by the quick release that play is removed. It will take you a few attempts to get this right but it must be done if you want your new bearings to last more than a few weeks.

11 Refit the gear cassette on to the splined freehub. The widest spline must align with the widest slot in the cassette. Refit any washer that was present, install the top sprocket (smallest) and then tighten the locknut with Shimano tool TL HG 15. The locknut should be quite tight, don't worry about the clicking noise when you tighten it, those teeth are there to stop it coming loose.

JARGON

FREEHUB/FREEWHEEL – a mechanism for allowing drive to be transmitted while pedalling, but which also allows the wheels to carry on turning without turning the cranks when the rider stops pedalling.

HUB – the unit at the centre of the wheel. It houses the wheel bearings and provides for spoke location via the flanges.

LOCKRING – the small threaded ring that holds the rear gear sprockets on a freehub.

PAWLS – small claw-like part inside a freewheel/freehub mechanism that engage with a toothed ring that rotates around them. In one direction they engage and drive can be transmitted, while in the other direction the ring is free to rotate and the pawls are pushed out of the way.

QUICK RELEASE/QR – a lever mechanism for fastening the wheel quickly and easily into the frame/forks. The QR runs through the wheel axle, and when the lever is closed it applies force between its

JARGON

⬅ ends in much the same way as tightening wheel nuts.

<u>SPLINE</u> – a method of joining two parts together so that they are rotationally linked. The gear sprockets on the Shimano freehub system are splined on to the freehub

Sprockets – a term used to describe the toothed sprockets of the rear gear cluster.

<u>TL-HG15, TL-PD40, TL-UN52, TL-FC20</u> – Shimano special tool code numbers (quote the appropriate one when buying a special tool).

<u>WD-40</u> – a penetrating oil used for freeing jammed fasteners, seat posts, stems, and so on. It is also very good at dispersing water – handy after you've washed the bike and you want to blast the water out of sensitive parts like the chain and gear/brake cables.

Hints 'n' tips

Grease

Grease all of the steel parts in a wheel hub including the quick release rod that slides through the axle. This is an often-neglected part and it can corrode quickly.

Bearings

Ball bearings can be bought, by the hundreds and fairly cheaply, from bearings stockists. Ball bearings from a source like this tend to be better quality than the ones you find pre-packaged in a bike shop – and having a stock of wheel bearings is a good idea anyway. Look in Yellow Pages under bearing stockists, give them a ring and tell them you want loose ball bearings, take one or two along with you (front and rear wheels are

different sizes sometimes) which they can then measure.

Washing

Do not jet wash against the seals of wheel hubs. These seals will only just stand the pressure of a regular garden hose, and even then it helps if you don't blast them directly – the force of the water can deform the seal and stop it sealing properly.

Often overlooked is the quick release - don't forget to grease it before refitting

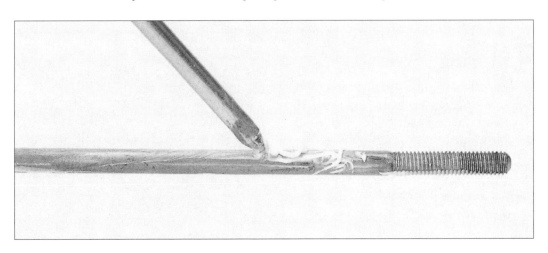

THE HEADSET

Introduction

Headsets take a lot of pounding so, if they develop a fault, this can rapidly cause major damage if left unattended.

A headset should turn smoothly with no tight spots, or play. The most common headset problem is looseness, and you often feel a knocking or clunking sensation when you are using the front brake. Once the headset starts doing this repeated impacts can soon wreck it. There's something wrong if the headset has tight spots too. Either the cups aren't seated in the frame properly or the cone on the fork is misaligned – or both.

JARGON

ALLEN KEY – hexagonal-shaped rod bent at 90° that fits into the head of an Allen bolt. Almost every bike uses Allen bolts.

CABLES – the wire system used to operate brakes and gears. Consisting of an inner section which is pulled (tension), and an outer section which is squeezed (compressed). Both inner and outer must be in good condition to operate under tension and compression.

CONE – the cone shaped part of a bearing assembly. Used with a cup and bearings.

DEGREASER – solvent which will remove grease. Useful for cleaning components,

The Headset

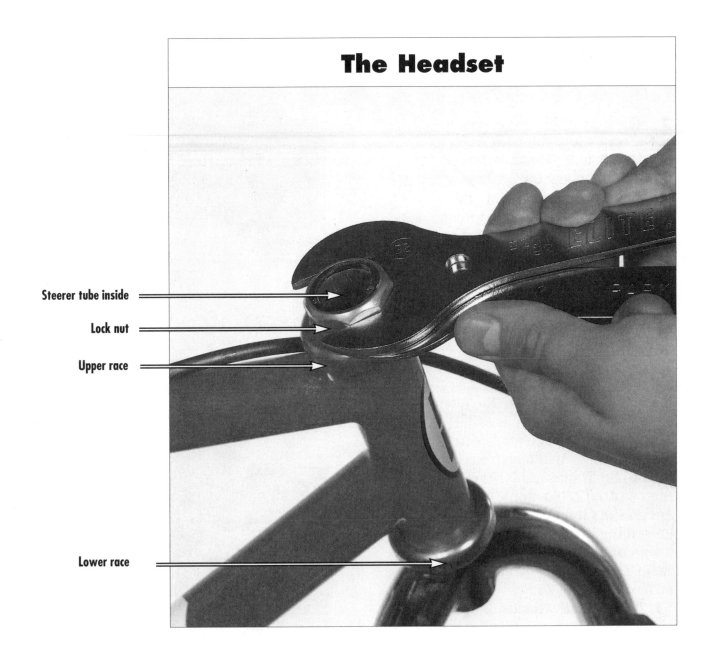

Steerer tube inside

Lock nut

Upper race

Lower race

Adjusting the Headset

1 The first step is to remove the stem by loosening the stem bolt. If this bolt is recessed then turn the Allen key the other way around (long end down into the stem) and place a piece of tubing or a ring spanner on the short end to provide the extra leverage.

2 Push down on the bolt to unseat the expander wedge from the bottom of the stem or unstick it if it has jammed in the steerer tube of the forks. If the stem still feels stuck then give the bolt a few good taps with a medium hammer – leave the Allen key in so as not to damage the head of the bolt. You may need to pull the cables that lead from the bars to the frame and forks out of their slotted cable stops, or if there are no slots it may be easier to loosen the brake and/or gear levers on the handle bar and jiggle them around until you can get the stem out.

3 To loosen the headset locknuts use two thin headset spanners. 1in headsets require 32mm, 1.125in require 36mm, and 1.25in require 40mm spanners. Loosen the top lock nut while holding the lower one (the top bearing cup). These should be quite tightly locked together and require considerable force to undo them initially.

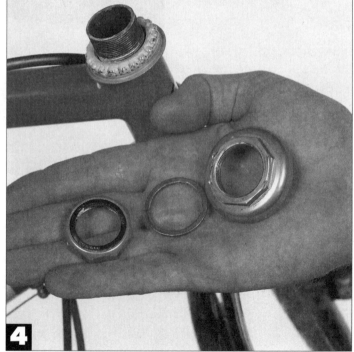

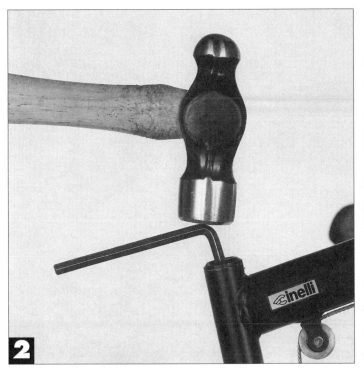

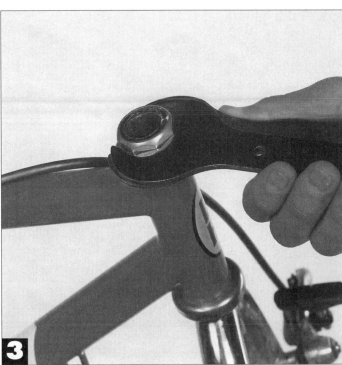

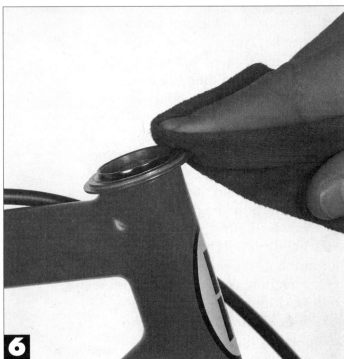

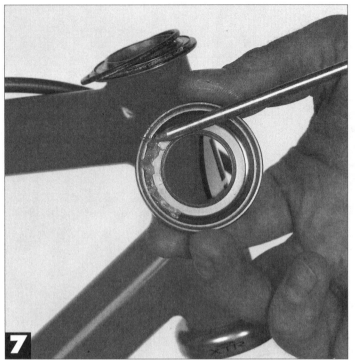

4 Remove the locknut and then the keyed washer or spacers (if any) and then unscrew the top bearing cup – holding the forks as you do so to stop them falling out of the frame. The bearings will stay in the top cup, stay on the top cone (or a mixture of both if they are loose bearings) or fall on the floor! Make a note of any seals and where and how they are fitted.

5 Lower the forks from the headtube of the frame, being careful not to lose any bearings. Once again make a note of seals and positions. Keep the bottom bearings separate from the top ones – they may well be of a different size.

6 Give everything a thorough wipe with a clean rag and

especially the chain when used with a chain cleaning tool.

EXPANDER WEDGE – a wedge-shaped piece of metal (usually aluminium) at the bottom of the stem quill (the part that goes into the fork steerer). When the expander bolt is tightened the wedge is pushed away from the stem and jams inside the steerer tube, holding the stem firmly to the forks.

HEADSET – the bearing assembly between the fork steerer and the headtube of the frame.

LOCTITE – name of company manufacturing, among other things, thread-locking compounds of varying strength.

STEERER TUBE – the tube coming from the forks that runs up inside the headtube of the frame .

THREAD-LOCKING COMPOUND – liquid applied to threads which sets anaerobically (without oxygen) to stop the fastener coming loose.

degreaser. Take a good look at the bearing surfaces in every part of the headset and at the bearings themselves.

The most common wear is caused by impact damage, which shows as small dents in the bearing surfaces, usually in the bottom bearing assembly. But any signs of permanent wear mean that the headset has lived its life and it is time for a new one.

7 Begin to re-assemble the headset with plenty of grease on all running surfaces.

8 Sometimes it pays to replace the ball bearings without the cage that carries them. This enables you to fit one or two more

bearings in which, in theory, helps to spread the load.

9 Re-assemble the headset by reversing steps 3 to 5. Hand tighten the top cup until you feel it tighten on the bearings and they start to bind a little. Next tighten the locknut down on to the top cup with a gentle nip of the spanner, then unscrew the top cup while holding the locknut with the other spanner. This locks the top cup and lock nut together and backs off the bearing pre-load just enough for them to run smoothly but with no play. You may have to repeat this procedure several times until you are happy with the adjustment.

Hints 'n' tips

Extra protection

Before you reassemble the headset cut a piece of old inner tube and slip it over the bottom cup that is pressed into the frame. Then put the forks back into the frame and roll it down to cover the bottom race assembly and stop crud and water getting in.

Thread lock

Use a thread-locking substance such as Loctite as extra prevention against the headset coming loose after you've adjusted and locked it up.

Extra protection; a piece of old inner tube can prevent water rusting your headset.

THE AHEADSET SYSTEM

Introduction

An Aheadset system doesn't differ that much from a conventional headset system, there are just a few less parts that's all. Instead of the stem inserting into a threaded steerer tube a non-threaded steerer tube inserts into an Aheadset-style stem (it has a clamp instead of a quill and wedge expander). The stem is then used to butt up against the top bearing to facilitate adjustment. A small expanding washer is inserted in the steerer into which a bolt running through a cap on top of the stem is threaded. When the bolt is tightened the stem pre-loads the bearing – in much the same way that you would just turn a conventional headset's top cup on a threaded steerer. Then all you do is tighten the bolts on the stem clamp and this holds the stem firmly on to the steerer tube.

  Of course, correct bearing adjustment depends upon the stem being able to slide smoothly up and down the steerer tube – so when the adjuster bolt in the cap at the top of the stem is tightened, the stem can move down the steerer and adjust the bearings.

The Aheadset System

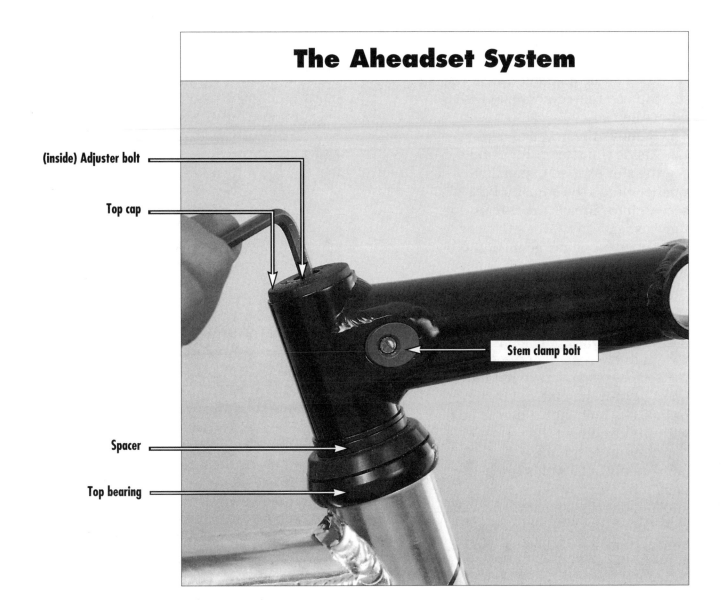

(inside) Adjuster bolt

Top cap

Stem clamp bolt

Spacer

Top bearing

Disassembly

1 Loosen the adjuster bolt in the top cap (anti-clockwise) with a 5mm Allen key.

2 Remove the bolt and cap. Inside the steerer tube you'll see the star-shaped expanding washer which the adjuster bolt screws into. Grease the threads in the washer. You'll notice that the steerer tube doesn't go all of the way to the top of the stem, it is necessary to have at least a 3mm gap between the top of the steerer and the top of the stem.

3 Loosen the stem clamp bolt/s (anti-clockwise) and remove the stem – remember to hold the forks or they may fall out of the frame. The bolt shown here is flush with the outside of the stem and operates an internal wedge system. Some people claim this is a better design because you don't get bolts sticking out (usually at the rear of the clamp) and mangling your knees. However, I've never banged my knee on any stem, and I've never met anyone who has – besides the headset cups stick out further than the bolts anyway!

4 The Aheadset system uses spacers to alter the height of the stem. By using a combination of spacers and different rise stems, handlebar position can be very finely tuned.

5 Some systems (Tioga most noticeably) have a circlip just above the top bearing which must

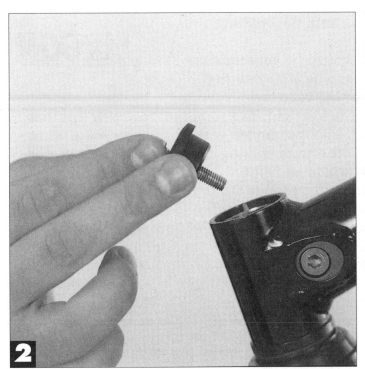

2

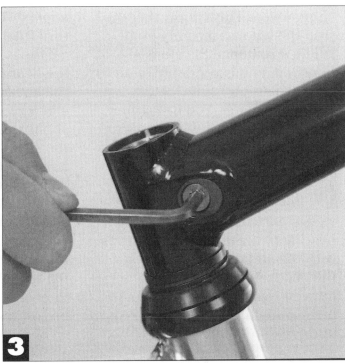

3

5

6

be removed. This is only there to stop the whole assembly from falling apart once the stem is removed, and is probably there to make assembly in the factory easier and faster. You can either refit it or replace it with a spacer of equivalent thickness upon re-assembly.

6 The top bearings assembly looks something like this. The wedge part seats into the top bearing to make sure that it turns with the steerer tube. The rest of the headset is the same as a conventional system and should be thoroughly cleaned and greased upon re-assembly.

Re-assembly

Assemble all of the parts on to the steerer tube in the order they were removed. Do not grease the area where the wedge touches the inside of the top bearing, just apply a light oil or chain lube at this point to prevent corrosion. Grease the steerer tube lightly and re-install the stem, top cap, and adjuster bolt.

Adjustment

Make sure the stem clamp bolt(s) are fully loose and the stem turns freely on the steerer tube. With the front of the bike off the ground tighten the adjuster bolt (clockwise) until the bearings begin to bind. Then loosen the adjuster bolt until the bearings turn freely.

If the bolt has to be very tight for the bearings to be adjusted then the interface between stem and steerer tube is too tight. The stem should form a light sliding fit with the steerer, otherwise bearing adjustment will be difficult.

The plastic cap on top of the stem is plastic for a reason and should not be replaced with an aftermarket alloy one. Plastic is used so that, if the unit is over tightened, the cap will break rather than other components. If the cap breaks this will be caused by an error on your part, or a failure in another part of the system (the stem won't push down on the top headset bearing).

Once the bearings have been adjusted, tighten the stem clamp bolt(s) fully using Loctite on the threads.

JARGON

AHEADSET – a relatively new method of pre-loading headset bearings with the use of a non-threaded fork steerer and a clamp on stem.

ALLEN KEY – hexagonal-shaped rod bent at 90° that fits into the head of an Allen bolt. Almost every bike uses Allen bolts.

CIRCLIP – small spring clip used to hold things together. It locates in a groove and must be held open or closed for removal and refitting.

HEADSET – the bearing assembly between the fork steerer and the headtube of the frame.

LOCTITE – name of company manufacturing, among other things, thread-locking compounds of varying strength.

LUBE/LUBRICANT, WET AND DRY – wet lubes stay wet to the touch when applied. Dry lubes evaporate to leave a dry film (usually teflon based). Wet lubes are good for wet conditions, while dry lubes are good for dusty conditions because they don't attract dirt.

Hints 'n' tips

JARGON

STEERER TUBE – the tube coming from the forks that runs up inside the headtube of the frame.
TEFLON – (see also lubes) high pressure lubricant developed by Du Pont™.

Bearings

Just as with a regular headset you can junk the bearing cages and just fill the cups with loose bearings bought from a bearing stockist. Check Yellow Pages for your nearest supplier and take along a sample to ensure you get the correct size.

Extra seals

Fitting an aftermarket neoprene seal is a wise precaution on the lower bearing assembly. Alternatively you can cut a section of old inner tube and slip it over the bottom bearing when you strip and rebuild the headset. However, this tends to trap any water that does find it's way in.

THE PEDALS

Introduction

Pedals have to stand up to a lot of abuse. They have to support the rider's weight, yet have bearings that are small and light and able to survive the water and mud thrown out by the front wheel.

Problems usually show themselves as roughness of the bearings, slack or wobbly pedals, and clicking noises when pedalling. Hardly anything ever goes wrong with a pedal that doesn't involve the bearings, so it helps to have some idea of what size ball bearings are needed to service them and buy a stock in advance.

JARGON

ALLEN KEY – hexagonal-shaped rod bent at 90° that fits into the head of an Allen bolt. Almost every bike uses Allen bolts.

CRANK ARMS – the arms that come out from the bottom bracket and which carry the pedals.

CONE – the cone shaped part of a bearing assembly. Used with a cup and bearings.

DEGREASER – solvent which will remove grease. Useful for cleaning components, especially the chain when used with a chain cleaning tool.

The Pedals

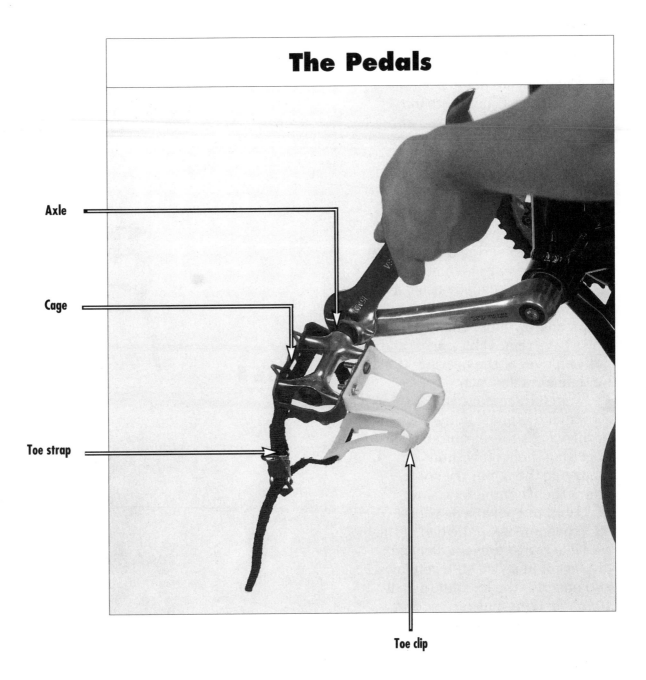

Axle

Cage

Toe strap

Toe clip

Servicing

1 Unscrew the pedal from the crank arm. The righthand pedal has righthand thread and unscrews anti-clockwise. The lefthand pedal has lefthand thread and unscrews clockwise.

2 Remove any clips and toe straps fitted and then check to see if the pedal cage hinders access to the bearing dust cap. If it does, and the cage is removable, then remove it (usually using a screwdriver or Allen key). Unfortunately most cheap pedals don't have removable cages, and if you can't get at the bearings it may be time for a new pair.

3 Carefully remove the dustcap from the pedal body. With old or dirty caps there is often no way of getting them off without damaging them, but try not to wreck them completely.

4 Hold the pedal axle with a spanner (wrap the end of the axle in a rag to prevent damage), or place it in a vice with soft jaws, and unscrew the locknut (usually 10mm or 12mm) using a socket spanner. Put the locknut in a safe place – replacements can be hard to find.

5 Remove the tabbed washer after the locknut by either rocking it side to side with two small screwdrivers or tip the pedal on its end and tap it gently on the floor. Put the washer in the same place as the locknut – these are

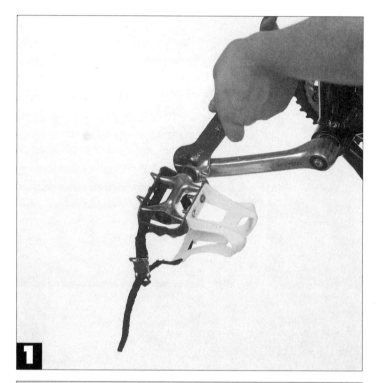

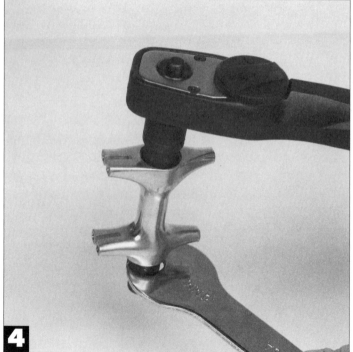

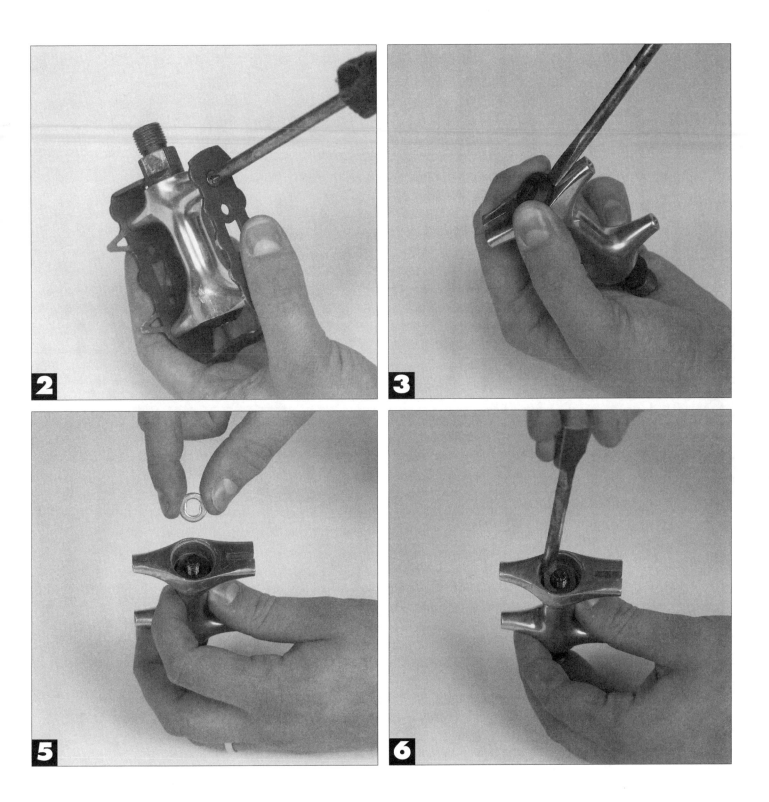

even harder to buy and pedal adjustment without one is a hassle.

6 Removing the bearing cone is sometimes a fiddly job, so here's the easy way. Place a flat bladed screwdriver between the flat of the cone and the side of the pedal body and then rotate the axle. Hold the pedal over a container to catch any bearings that may fall out.

7 Hold the axle over a container to catch stray bearings and then pull the axle from the pedal body. Don't throw the bearings away because you'll need to take them to the shop for comparison when you go to buy new ones.

8 Thoroughly clean everything with degreaser and rags. Every speck of dirt and grease must be removed before you can properly check for wear. You can often get away with spindles or pedals that are only very slightly pitted, but if this is the case, you know it will be time for replacement parts or new pedals the next time they cause you problems.

9 Grease the bearing running surface just enough to make the ball bearings stick in place and then put the bearings in. Once they're all in place put more grease in over them.

10 Slide the axle into the pedal body and push it in until it sits on the bearings evenly. There should be enough grease in the pedal so that it is squeezed out when you push in the spindle.

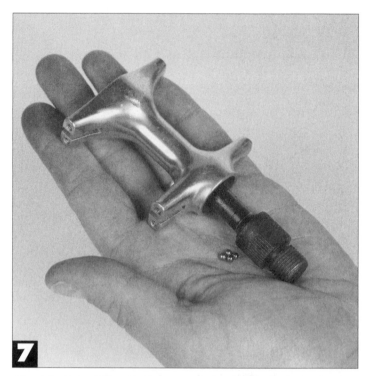

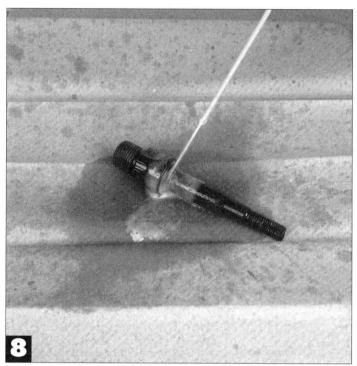

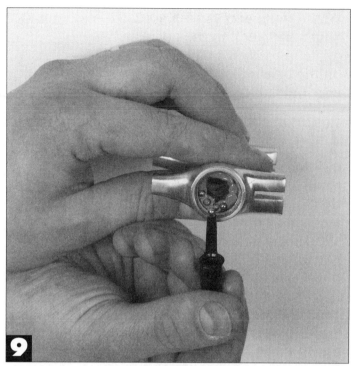

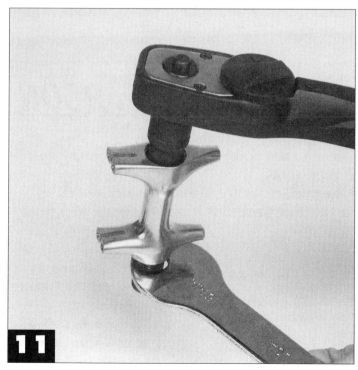

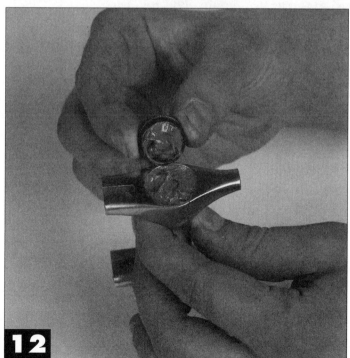

Wipe off the excess with your finger and put it in the pedal dustcap ready for step 12. Screw on the bearing cone, tab washer, and locknut.

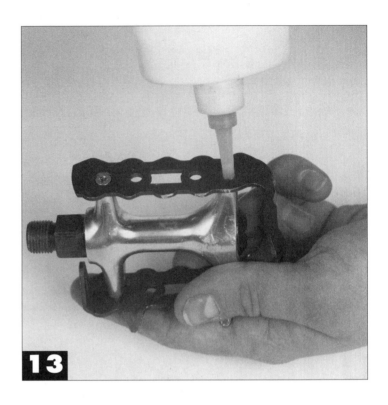

11 Adjust the bearing by using the flat-bladed screwdriver method (see step 6) until there is a small amount of play. Next fully tighten the locknut using the method from step 4 and check the axle to see if there is any bearing play or tightness of rotation. If the bearing is tight, loosen the locknut and loosen the bearing cone a very small amount with the flat-bladed screwdriver. Fully tighten the locknut and check axle play and pedal rotation again. The reverse applies for a loose bearing. Expect to fiddle about with adjustment at least three or four times before it's correct – no play and smooth rotation.

12 Pack the dust cap and the outer bearing with grease and push it back into the pedal. This should push grease through the outer bearing and you should repeat this until grease is pushed out of the inboard bearing.

13 To prevent the cage bolts from vibrating loose, put a few drops of Loctite thread lock (242) on them.

14 Refit the clips and straps using the biggest washers that will fit between the bolts and clips. Use Nyloc nuts or a conventional nut with a spring washer and thread lock, to prevent them coming loose.

15 Before refitting the pedals to the crank, make sure the threads are clean to the point of being sterile, then grease the threads and the surface where the pedal butts up against the crank arm.

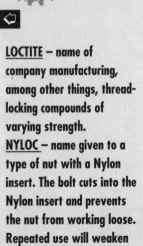

JARGON

LOCTITE – name of company manufacturing, among other things, thread-locking compounds of varying strength.

NYLOC – name given to a type of nut with a Nylon insert. The bolt cuts into the Nylon insert and prevents the nut from working loose. Repeated use will weaken the locking power of the Nylon insert.

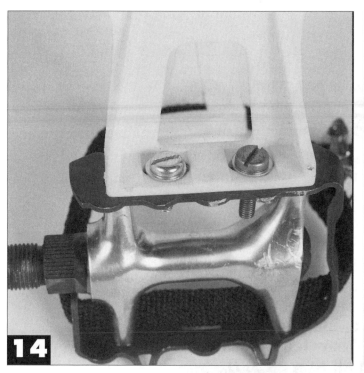

14

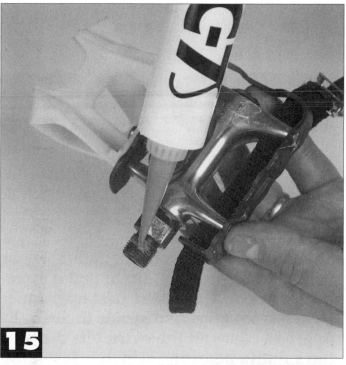

15

Hints 'n' tips

Straps

Use a zip tie to hold the strap against the pedal cage. This gives greater clearance for mud to fall through and also prevents the strap from pulling through the cage. Set the strap buckle next to the cage before tightening the zip tie.

Cheap grease injection

You can make a simple grease injection system that will work with the current style of pointed tipped grease guns. Simply drill a

hole (you can use a small screwdriver on plastic dustcaps) in the dust cap just big enough to allow the tip of the grease gun to fit in. Then all it takes to grease the pedal is a quick pump or two until grease oozes out of the inboard bearing.

NEW PEDALS
When you buy a new set of pedals the first thing you should do is pull them apart and

grease them as shown here. Quite often the grease put in there by the manufacturers isn't worth the effort it takes to wipe it off.

SPD PEDALS

Introduction

Shimano SPD (Shimano Pedalling Dynamics) pedals are by far the most popular clip-in pedal system on the mountain bike market. Almost the first upgrade people make is a switch from clips and straps to SPDs. But along with that upgrade come all the extra bits that need servicing beside the spindle bearings, which is just about all that an SPD pedal has in common with a normal pedal.

SPD pedals, for those who don't know, require the use of a special shoe that has a special cleat on its sole. This cleat engages in the pedal by pushing aside a spring-loaded hinge that then springs back and catches behind a lip on the cleat securing the shoe to the pedal. Twisting the shoe forces the cleat to run up against angled ramps on the body plate of the pedal and also against the angled side of the catch plates on the hinge. This action releases the cleat from the pedal.

SPDs come in two main types the PD-M737 which has hinges both on the front and the rear of the pedal, and the PD-M535 which has only one hinge at the rear of the pedal. Both pedals are double sided and work on the same principle with the same cleats. The PD-M535 is cheaper and weighs slightly less, but the way that the cleat engages in the pedal is slightly different. With the 535 the front of the cleat has to slide under the catch plate before the rear presses the hinge out of the way. With the 737 there is a hinge front and rear, so it doesn't matter which end goes in first, often all that is required of the rider is to stand on the pedal and it will engage both ends.

SPD Pedals

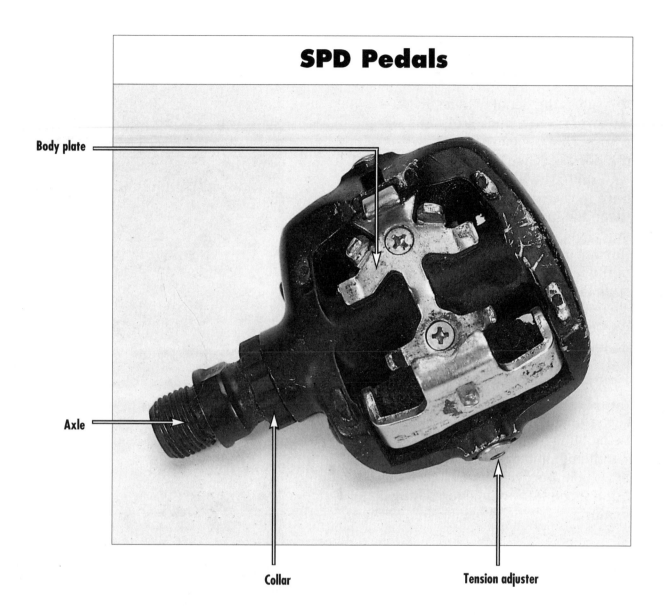

Body plate

Axle

Collar

Tension adjuster

Regular cleaning and lubrication

1 Clean the pedal with a stiff
brush and a bucket of water or
a hose. Don't blast the pedal with
the hose because this will force
water into the bearings and you'll
have to do a complete service.
Clean the inside of the pedal as
much as possible, try and get all of
the dirt and grit out of the springs
of the hinge inside the pedal. A
squirt of degreaser often helps to
clean the springs but don't let it
get near the end of the axle where
it can find its way into the
bearings.

2 Use a thick liquid lube on all of
the hinge pivots and also on
the springs. The lube should resist
being flung off and be water
repellent. I find the best lube for
SPDs is motorcycle chain lube –
but not the O-Ring type for O-Ring
chains.

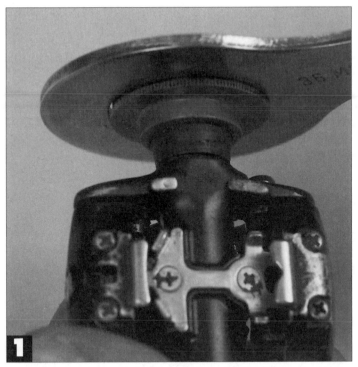

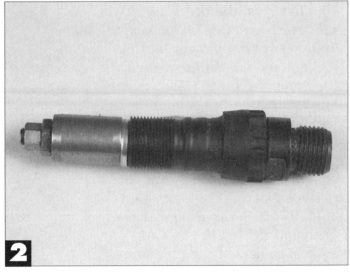

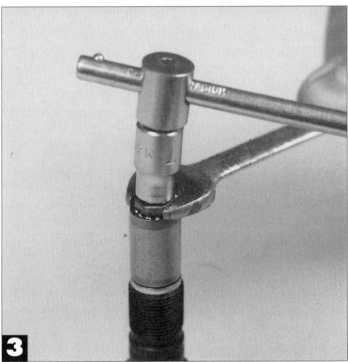

Servicing bearings

1 Remove the pedal from the crank (anti-clockwise for the righthand pedal and clockwise for the lefthand pedal) with a 15mm spanner or a 6mm Allen key, which fits in the rear of the spindle. Unscrew the plastic collar on the inside of the pedal by turning the special tool TL-PD40 (usually supplied with the pedals) the opposite direction to that shown by the arrow labelled 'tighten' on the plastic collar.

2 The axle unit will then unscrew from the body of the pedal. The bearing unit is the silver tube at the end of the axle. Very small ball bearings are held at either end of this tube, with the outermost bearing having a cone and a locknut with which to adjust bearing play.

3 To adjust the bearing you will need: for PD-M737 pedals, a 7mm socket or spanner for the locknut and a 10mm spanner for the cone; and for PD-M535 pedals, an 8mm socket or spanner for the locknut and a 11mm spanner for the cone.

Hold the axle either with a spanner or an Allen key and loosen (anti-clockwise) the locknut on the end. Adjust the bearing with the cone and tighten the locknut against it. Repeat the procedure until there is no play in the bearings and they turn smoothly.

4 The simplest way to grease an SPD pedal is to fill the inside of the pedal body (after cleaning) with about three-quarters of an inch of grease. Then when the axle unit is re-installed the grease is forced through the bearing unit, between the collar and the axle. This ensures the maximum amount of grease is present and also forms a pretty effective shield against the ingress of dirt and water.

5 When the collar is being tightened, grease must be forced out through the gap between it and the axle. If grease does not emerge unscrew the collar and put more grease in the pedal body until it does. It's a bit messy, but it's the best way.

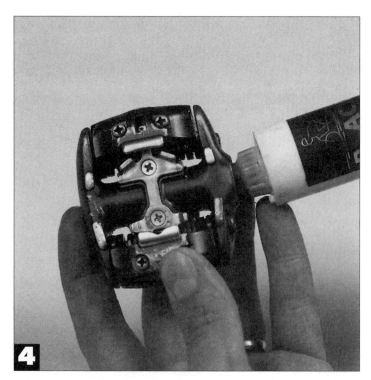

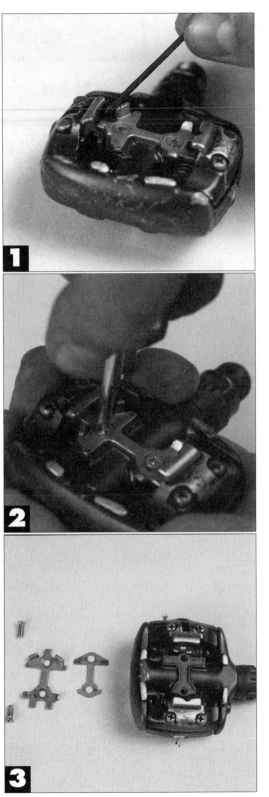

Body plate replacement

1 Look inside the pedal for the end of the tension adjuster bolt. Loosen the adjuster (anti-clockwise, 3mm Allen key) until it nearly unscrews from the small plate it locates in. This allows the hinge part of the pedal to loosen up enough to get the body plates off. Be careful not to unscrew the tension adjuster bolt all of the way out of the small plate.

2 Unscrew the two screws holding the body plates on. All of the small crosshead screws on an SPD are Phillips No 2, so it pays to buy a good Phillips screwdriver. The screws will be quite tight so push down as hard as possible on the screwdriver while turning it anti-clockwise to prevent it slipping out and damaging the screws.

3 Under the body plate is a thin shim, do not lose it or mix it up with the one from the other side. When a new top plate is fitted, the shim must be refitted in its original position. Use thread locking compound when refitting the two screws. Loose body plate screws in the middle of a ride are a real pain.

Hints 'n' tips

First time SPD users

For those new to the idea of fastening your feet to the pedals Shimano offer a multi-release cleat – the SM-SH55. This allows you to disengage from the pedals by pulling your feet upwards as well as the usual twisting motion to release the cleat.

Shoe screws

The screws that hold the cleat on the sole of the shoe are often neglected. Keep an eye on them because over a period of time they can seize, thus rendering the shoe useless. Loosen the screws (one at a time so as not to disturb the cleat position) at least once a month and grease the threads and the tapered area that fits into the cleat.

Cleat care

After muddy rides it pays to scrape all of the mud away from the cleats, hose them down with water and then give them a quick spray with a water repellent such as WD40. A clean and rust free cleat will last longer and do less harm to the pedals.

Release tension

Brand new SPDs have the release tension set somewhere between a quarter and half. In the instructions it states that the loosest tension is just before the little red dot disappears from the small 'window' (actually a square hole). In fact the release tension can be slackened further. Look inside the pedal for the end of the tension adjuster bolt and you will see it screws into a small plate. The tension can be backed off up to the point where the bolt is in danger of coming out of the plate. Keep at least one full thread showing and things will be just fine. You'll find this is much better if you are new to SPD pedals, because the lower release tension can make the difference between a crash or just an embarrassing stumble.

JARGON

DEGREASER – solvent which will remove grease. Useful for cleaning components, especially the chain when used with a chain cleaning tool.

LUBE/LUBRICANT, WET AND DRY – wet lubes stay wet to the touch when applied. Dry lubes evaporate to leave a dry film (usually teflon based). Wet lubes are good for wet conditions, while dry lubes are good for dusty conditions because they don't attract dirt.

SPDs – Shimano Pedalling Dynamics. A method of fastening the rider's foot to the pedal via a small cleat, screwed to the shoes, which clips into the pedal mechanism.

SPINDLE – a part upon which another part rotates. For example a pedal spindle is the part which screws into the crank arm and round which the pedal rotates.

TEFLON – (see also lubes) high pressure lubricant developed by Du Pont™ TL-PD20, TL-HG15, TL-FC40, TL-UN52 – Shimano special tool code

JARGON

numbers (quote the appropriate one when buying a special tool). <u>WD-40</u> – a penetrating oil used for freeing jammed fasteners, seat posts, stems, and so on. It is also very good at dispersing water – handy after you've washed the bike and you want to blast the water out of sensitive parts like the chain and gear/brake cables.

Use a 3mm allen key to adjust new SPDs to your own preferred setting.

THE HANDLEBAR
STEM AND BAR ENDS

Introduction

These days, with the weight of handlebars getting lower and the thickness of the tubing walls getting thinner, it is important that your handlebar is fitted correctly. Do not scratch your handlebar! A scratch leads to a concentration of stress and, if the load is concentrated in that area, it will probably fail – scratches near the stem clamp area are especially bad news.

When new, most bars are strong enough to stand up to the punishment dished out by the hardest mountain bikers, but as a bar is repeatedly loaded and unloaded its strength decreases – so older bars tend to be weaker.

From this we can see that it makes sense to reduce the stress on a handlebar and thus extend its life. Aside from keeping the bar free from scratches and gouges, take a look at the clamps that go around the bar. Where there is a sharp edge against the surface of the bar take a fine file and round off the edge.

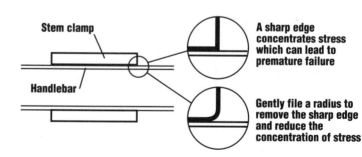

Stem clamp

Handlebar

A sharp edge concentrates stress which can lead to premature failure

Gently file a radius to remove the sharp edge and reduce the concentration of stress

The handlebar stem and bar ends

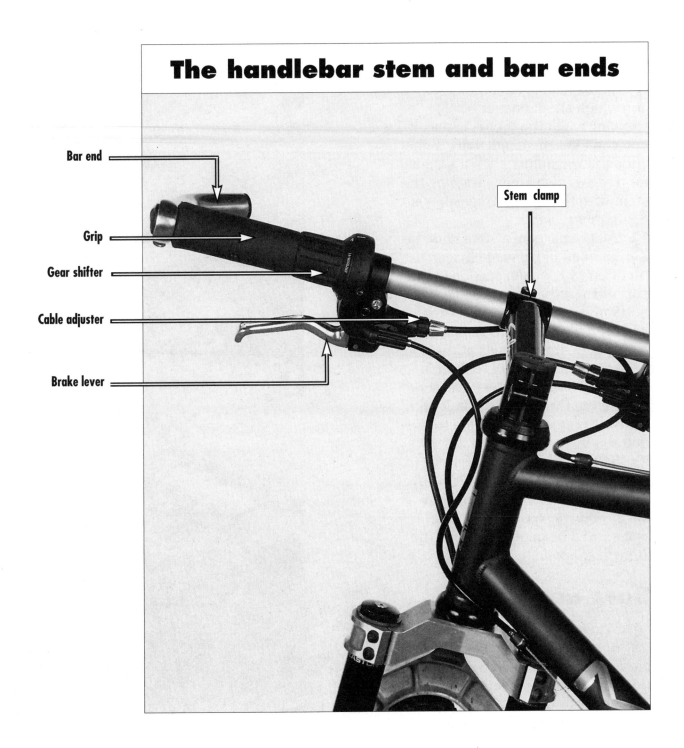

Bar end

Grip

Gear shifter

Cable adjuster

Brake lever

Stem clamp

Stems

1 Stems have a limit indicator which should never be showing when the bike is in use. If you can't get the handlebars high enough for comfort, then it's time for a higher rise stem – running the stem with the limit mark visible is dangerous.

2 All the parts of a stem must be greased to prevent corrosion. An often overlooked section is the part of the expander wedge that butts up against the stem. When you tighten the stem the wedge has to slide up the angle at the base of the stem – and to do this efficiently it must be well greased. Grease the threads of the bolt and also underneath the head of the bolt.

3 The stem should be tight enough so that you can't move it. Place the wheel between your knees and try to twist the bars, you should be unable to move the stem in the forks.

Bars and grips

4 When installing a handlebar it helps to prise open the stem clamp with a large screwdriver, but take great care not to scratch the handlebar or damage the stem. And don't force the handlebars into the stem by twisting them around.

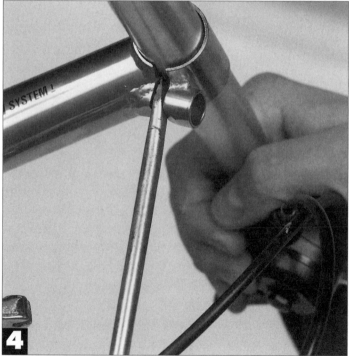

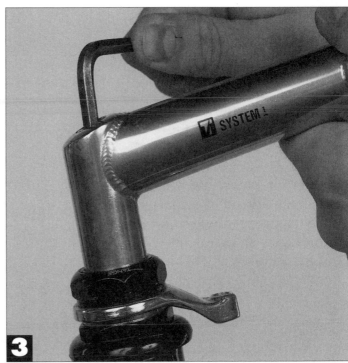

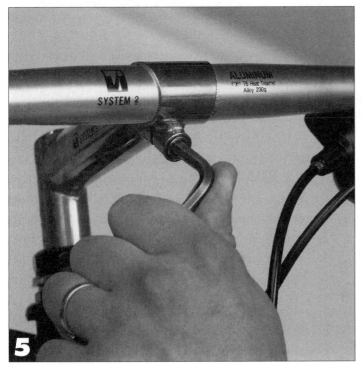

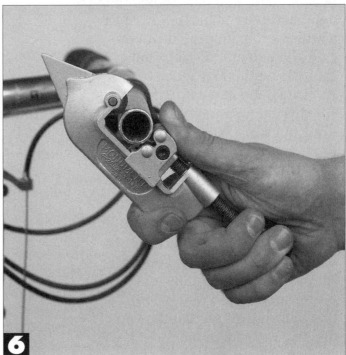

5 The stem clamp should be tight enough to stop the bars rotating and no more. Over-tight stem clamps can deform the handlebar and be the first step towards a sudden and potentially dangerous failure.

6 The best way to shorten handlebars is with a tube cutter, but a hacksaw will do the same job. File off any sharp edges after trimming. Always install bar end plugs – an open ended bar can cut surprisingly deeply into human flesh in a crash...

7 You can remove and install grips in several ways, but the easiest is to use hairspray! Spray a long thin screwdriver and insert it between grip and bar (remember, don't scratch the bar!). Now spray a little more hairspray down the grip and twist it off. To install grips the best method is, again, to use hairspray and leave it to dry, or car spray paint (gloss type) which dries quicker – 5 or 10 minutes.

Bar ends

8 If you want to make holes in the ends of your grips this is best done when the grip is off the bar – simply cut the end off with scissors or a sharp knife. **a)** For a neater looking job remove the bar end plug and gently tap the end of the grip with a hammer, which will cut a neat hole in the end of it. Don't hit the grip hard, use plenty of light taps, not a few heavy hits.

9 Don't over-tighten bar ends. They should be secure enough that they don't move when you are riding, but no tighter – thin-walled aluminium or carbon bars can easily be damaged by over-tight bar ends.

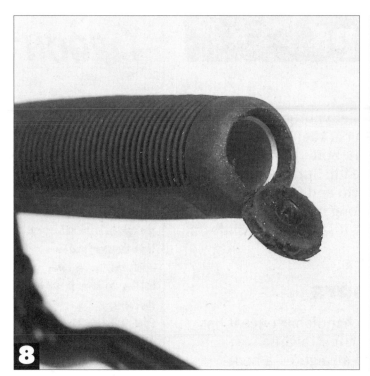

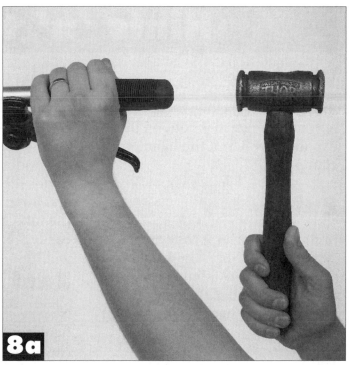

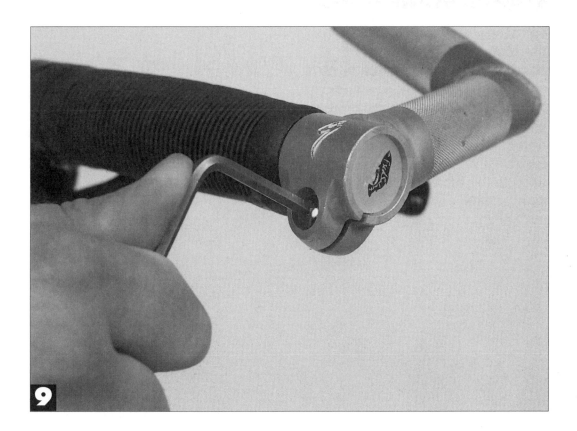

Hints 'n' tips

Washers

Always use a washer between the bolt and the stem – both on the expander bolt and the handlebar clamp bolt.

Bolts

Bolts work better if they are greased well. Not only should you grease the thread, but you should also grease under the head of the bolt, the part that presses against the washer.

Lightweight bolts

For safety reasons it is unwise to use aluminium bolts in the handlebar clamp or bar ends. Most aluminium bolts have just under half the strength of a similar steel bolt, and a failed handlebar clamp bolt can cause a serious crash. However, aluminium bolts can be used in the brake lever and shifter clamp bolts.

Grips

If you can't get your grips off, never try to cut them off with a knife – you're bound to scratch the bar underneath. Spray a lube under the grip and twist it back and forth along its length to work the lube in – it should then slide off easily.

Bent bars

Never use a handlebar once it has bent, replace it straight away. Never try to straighten a bent handlebar either, you'll just weaken it further.

JARGON

EXPANDER WEDGE – a wedge-shaped piece of metal (usually aluminium) at the bottom of the stem quill (the part that goes into the fork steerer). When the expander bolt is tightened the wedge is pushed away from the stem and jams inside the steerer tube, holding the stem firmly to the forks.

LUBE/LUBRICANT, WET AND DRY – wet lubes stay wet to the touch when applied. Dry lubes evaporate to leave a dry film (usually teflon based). Wet lubes are good for wet conditions, while dry lubes are good for dusty conditions because they don't attract dirt.

TEFLON – (see also lubes) high pressure lubricant developed by Du Pont™

BOLTS - Threads need lubrication to keep them tight and prevent corrosion and seizure.

THE SADDLE
AND SEAT POST

Introduction

Saddles

Seats should be chosen with only one thing in mind – comfort. Weight is a consideration for obsessive weight freaks, but comfort should be the governing factor. It might seem a good idea to save a few grams but, if you find you can't spend more than 20 minutes in the saddle without getting sore, then you've made a very poor choice.

Luckily most lightweight saddles are now as comfortable, if not more so, than their heavier, standard counterparts.

Saddles specifically designed for women have improved over recent years too, mainly because most of them are now designed by women for women. By far the most popular and highly-rated women's saddles are those designed by Georgina Terry. They have a perforated hull section towards the front of the seat that reduces uncomfortable pressure, and there are several versions available – all featuring the same design ideas and excellent construction.

Seat posts

The seat post is a simple item, but its dimensions are very important. The diameters of seat posts start at 25.4mm and range up to 32.6mm in 0.2mm increments. Therefore it is crucial that your seat post is exactly the right size for your frame. You might not even notice that your seat post is too small, but if you are 0.2mm under size this can cause damage to both frame and post. Look for a slightly tight, sliding fit –

Saddle and seat post

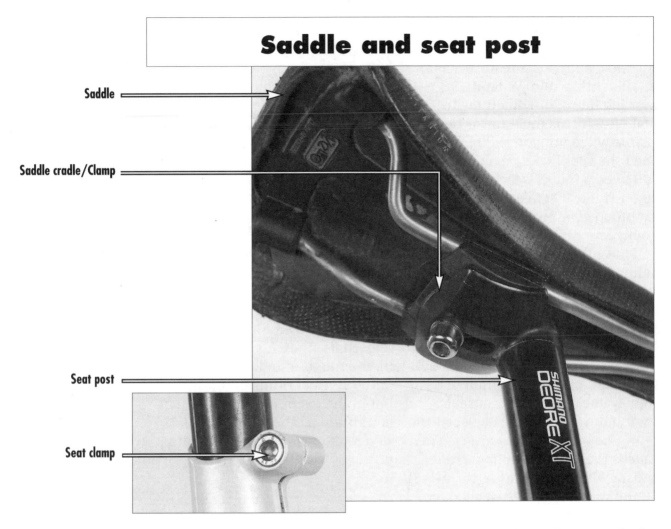

Saddle

Saddle cradle/Clamp

Seat post

Seat clamp

not so tight as to require twisting to raise or lower it, and not so slack that it drops down by itself.

Seat post length varies from about 300mm to 400mm – but the actual useable length depends upon how much you have inserted in the frame. For reasons of strength it's best to have at least 2cm of post below the area of the frame where the top tube joins the seat tube. Measure from the top of the seat tube to where the underneath of the top tube joins it, add 2cm to this length and you will have the minimum amount of seat post required. Any less than this and the seat cluster area of the frame will not be correctly supported, which could lead to failure over a period of time. If you find you need more than 300mm of exposed post then your frame is almost certainly one size too small.

Seat post

1 Most seat posts feature a 'max height', a 'min', a 'limit' warning line… or something to that effect. This must never be visible when you are riding. If you need the seat higher than this then you need a longer seat post or a larger frame. On bikes with extended seat tubes (like Kona or Rocky Mountain) make sure that you have at least 2cm of post below the point where the top tube joins the seat tube.

2 A good coating of grease on the seat post is essential, because it stops water finding its way down the seat tube and into the frame. The combination of a steel frame, an aluminium seat post and water makes an electrical cell – like a very weak battery. This causes the aluminium to corrode and, in winter conditions, the salt on the roads that gets washed into the seat tube makes things even worse. This corrosion builds up on the surface of the aluminium seat post, takes up any space between the seat post and the frame, and the post then becomes well and truly jammed in the frame. Regular cleaning and greasing prevents this, and also helps you keep an eye out for corrosion inside the seat tube – shine a torch down inside the frame.

3 The saddle clamp bolt in the top of the post also needs a generous application of grease.

Because some seat posts have strange threads and even weirder bolts, spares can be hard to find, so take care of the one you've got – it's a wise precaution. Grease under the head of the bolt too, and don't lose the washer – they too are usually an odd size and finding a replacement can be difficult.

Seat post clamps

Most production bikes now have aluminium seat quick releases or steel bolts. Whatever your bike has, it's important to keep it clean and well greased. Don't over tighten it either. It should be just tight enough to hold the seat post under normal riding conditions – but in the event of a crash it may just rotate a little and prevent severe damage to both seat and post.

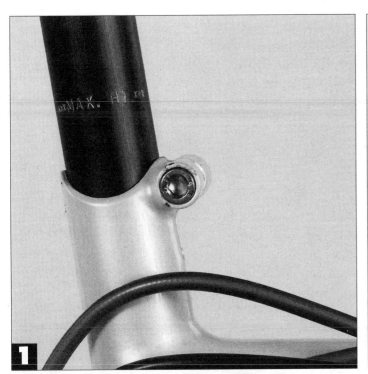

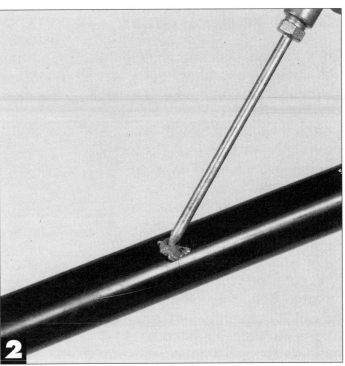

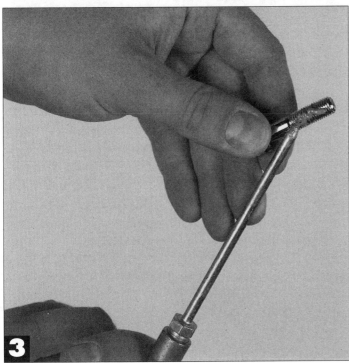

Seat rail clamps

1 The most common method of holding a saddle in place is with a single bolt cradle. One large bolt clamps an upper cradle plate on to the lower one with the seat rails trapped between. The lower cradle usually has a grooved surface that mates with a similar surface on top of the seat post. The main disadvantage of this system is that it doesn't offer fine adjustment of saddle angle because the grooves are quite coarse. Keep the bolt greased and check it frequently for tightness.

2 Twin bolt clamps offer probably the finest adjustment of any post. You can alter the angle of the seat by loosening one bolt slightly and tightening the other. With this design the seat post is often lighter because of the much smaller cradle design. The downside to this is that the clamp is placed directly above the seat post. This is fine if you have enough rearwards adjustment available with the saddle rails, but if not then the distance between saddle and handlebars, and more importantly the saddle position relative to the cranks, is reduced.

3 A few seat posts use a cylindrical cradle clamped by a two-bolt hinge. This system provides excellent saddle angle adjustment, and with the cradle set rearwards as in a regular single-bolt post. Keep the bolts clean and well greased and make sure that they are both tightened by the same amount. If one is tighter than the other the looser one may vibrate free.

JARGON

QUICK RELEASE/QR – a lever mechanism for fastening the wheel quickly and easily into the frame/forks. The QR runs through the wheel axle, and when the lever is closed it applies force between its ends in much the same way as tightening wheel nuts.

SADDLE RAILS – the two rails underneath the saddle which locate into the seat post clamp on top of the seat post.

SEAT POST – the post that fits into the seat tube of the frame and has the seat fastened to the top of it.

SEAT TUBE – the part of the frame that the seat post fits into.

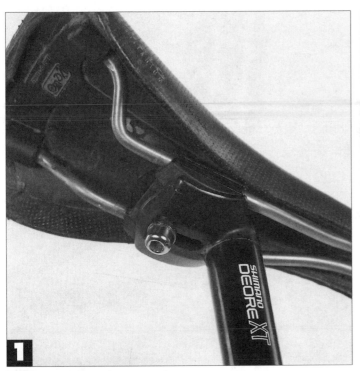

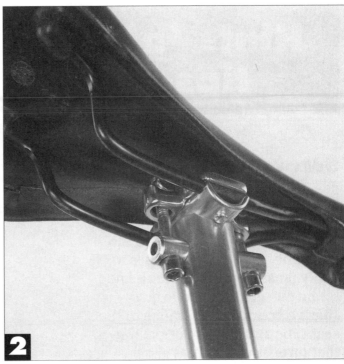

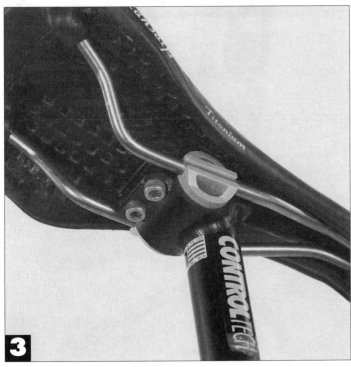

Hints 'n' tips

Scratches

If the seat post is the right size for the frame but it gets scratched while it is being inserted into the seat tube, then the problem is a badly finished frame. Using a fine round file, gently remove any sharp edges at the entrance to the seat tube and the slot at the top that forms the clamp.

Bent bolts

If the seat post clamp bolt or quick release (QR) bends when you tighten it, the seat post is either too small or the clamp or frame is of poor quality. On some Taiwanese frames the seat clamp (either built-in or a separate) can be of poorer quality. If the clamp is a separate item, try to find a better-quality replacement. If the clamp is part of the frame there is not much you can do.

Extra seal

A piece of old inner tube cut to length, pulled over the seat clamp, smeared with silicon grease, and then rolled up over the clamp and post will serve as an extra defence

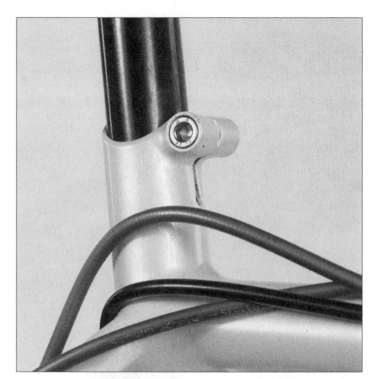

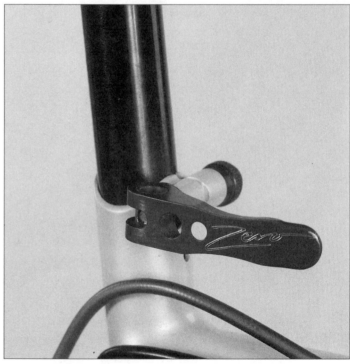

POST CLAMPS - Heavy steel quick releases have all but disappeared from production mountain bikes and have given way to lightweight aluminium QR's (bottom) or bolts (top).

against the ingress of water. Don't leave it too long between regreasing though because the inner tube will trap any water that does get under it.

Mystery creaks

On Control Post seat posts the seat rail can sometimes rub against the front of the hinge part of the clamp. This will result in a dull metallic clicking noise that seems to originate anywhere but the seat post. Grease between all the surfaces of a seat post and the seat.

Light bolts

Alloy and poor grade titanium bolts are a big no-no as far as the seat area is concerned. Nasty accidents can occur when alloy bolts fail, and it just isn't worth the pain and embarrassment for the few grams they save.

Seized posts

If the seat post gets jammed in the frame then remove the seat clamp bolt or QR and soak as much penetrating oil down the seat tube as possible. Gently tapping the top of the post with a wooden mallet can sometimes free a jammed post. It doesn't matter that you're trying to hit it into the frame, just so long as it moves.

If you are not too concerned about saving the post, then clamp it in a vice and try turning the frame, but be careful with lightweight frames.

GETTING YOUR WHEELS TRUE

Introduction

As long as mountain bike wheels are 26in in diameter, and only have 32 spokes, they will bend... A wheel that size, with so few spokes, can only take a certain amount of abuse. Small wobbles are a common sight after a hard ride and, if you crash, the wheel may be quite badly bent, so knowing how to straighten a wheel is important.

Whether you're moving the rim a few millimetres, or an inch or more, the technique is the same. A wheel-trueing stand isn't vital, although you do get better results with one. Taping or blue-tacking small Allen keys to the frame will do more or less the same job and once you've got the hang of things you can straighten a wheel quite rapidly out on the trail.

Wheel truing

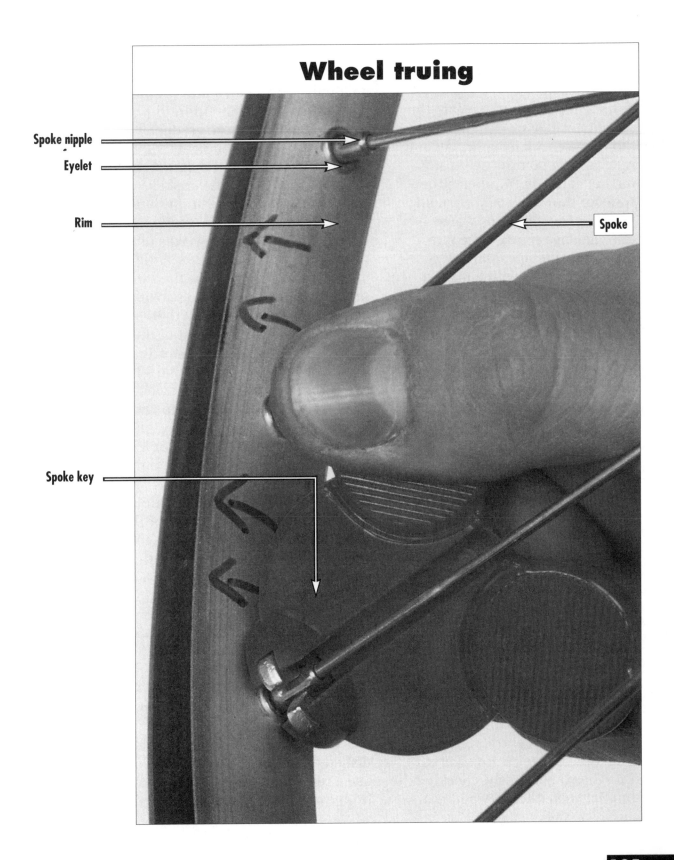

Spoke nipple

Eyelet

Rim

Spoke

Spoke key

Wheel Truing

1 It's important to prepare the job properly. With the wheel in the frame check for any play in the hub bearing before you go any further. If this is OK, then either transfer the wheel to the trueing stand or leave it in the frame – after having removed the tyre, tube, and rim tape. Mark all of the big inaccuracies with a marker pen to start with.

2 If you've broken a spoke you'll have to take the wheel to a good bike shop for a replacement. When you replace a spoke, copy the existing pattern and make sure that the spoke heads alternate left and right of the hub flange. Don't bend the spoke before fitting, but don't be afraid to bend it once you've passed it through the hole in the hub flange to get it into the hole in the rim. Oil the thread on the end of the spoke and fit the nipple, screwing it down until it is lightly tensioned.

3 If you're using the frame to true the wheel then use the brake blocks as a reference to check for side-to-side movement, and tape or stick an Allen key above the rim to check for up-and-down movement. Wheels are easier and quicker to true if the up and down (concentric) inaccuracies are removed first. Spin the wheel slowly, checking the gap between Allen key and rim.

Where the gap gets bigger make a note of whether this happens suddenly or is just a shallow dip. A sudden flat spot will require rim replacement, but more gradual flat spots can be 'squeezed out'.

Mark the start and the end of the flat spot and loosen the spokes (anti-clockwise) between these two points a quarter of a turn each. Tighten the rest of the spokes until the dip is squeezed out.

With high spots you use the same procedure but tighten the spokes along the high spot to pull that section in line with the rest of the wheel. After this it often helps to loosen all of the spokes a quarter of a turn. Don't worry about wheel dish yet, just get rid of the up and down bits first.

4 Once the wheel is more or less round it's time to get rid of the side to side inaccuracies. If the drive side (gear sprocket) of the rim touches the brake block, or the pointer of a trueing stand, loosen the drive side spokes along the length of the bend a quarter of a turn and tighten the non-drive side a quarter of a turn. If the rim has gone too far tighten the drive side spokes slightly, check the bend, and either tighten a little more or loosen them off a little. Reverse the procedure if the non-drive side is bent.

To ensure the wheel is correctly dished, place it in the frame and use a ruler to measure the distance from each side of the rim to the

chainstays/fork legs. Tighten the nipples on the side furthest away from the chainstay/fork legs a quarter of a turn (on the drive side of the rear wheel turn the spokes an eighth of a turn). If it is still out of dish, loosen the spokes on the side closest to the chainstay/fork leg. The idea is not to lose too much tension, but to centre the wheel in the frame. Once you get the hang of things it becomes a lot easier.

5 Once the wheel has been trued, everything has to be bedded in a little. To do this place the end of the axle on the floor and push down on the rim, working around the rim at six inch intervals. You should hear pinging noises from the spokes as everything settles down.

6 Check the wheel again because step 5 can cause slight imperfections. Check that there are no spokes protruding through the nipple heads. If there are you'll have to remove that spoke and either cut or file it shorter before replacing it. Fit the rim tape, tyre, and tube, and refit the wheel to the bike. Check the brake blocks are adjusted correctly, and you're done.

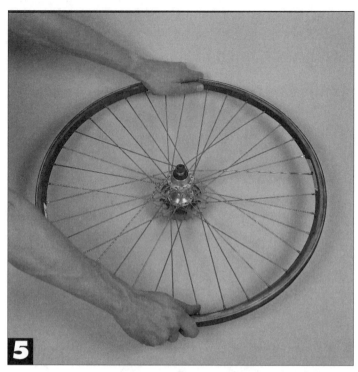

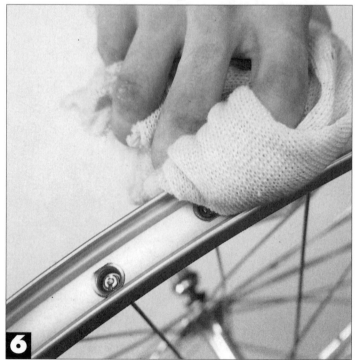

JARGON

ALLEN KEY – hexagonal-shaped rod bent at 90° that fits into the head of an Allen bolt. Almost every bike uses Allen bolts.

FLANGE – the part of the hub the spokes thread through.

SPOKE KEY – tool for turning the spoke nipples of a wheel so that the spoke tension can be adjusted.

SPROCKETS – a term used to describe the toothed sprockets of the rear gear cluster.

TYRE BEADS – the part of the tyre that locates into the wheel rim. Standard tyres have a bead made from steel wire while lighter, more expensive tyres use Kevlar.

If you badly taco your wheels (so they go crisp shaped) you're in need of a new rim anyway, so it doesn't matter if you damage it further to get you home.

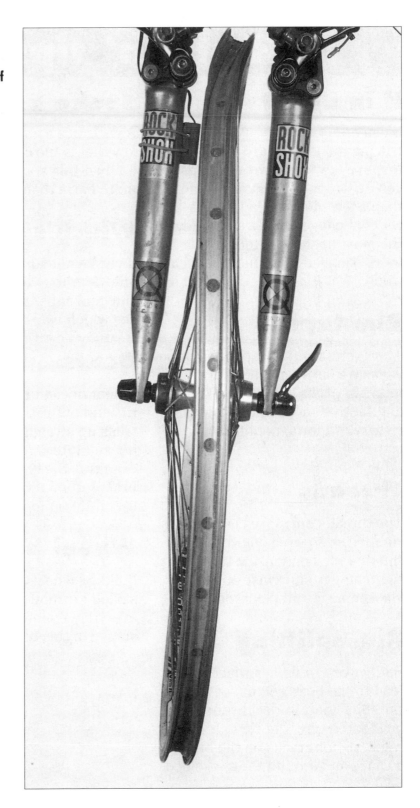

Hints 'n' tips

If in doubt

If you aren't sure about wheel trueing then leave it to a bike shop. A spoke key in the wrong hands can do irreparable damage in less than a few minutes. In fact it is widely believed that a spoke key is the most dangerous tool an inexperienced cycle mechanic can own!

Rim tape

The lightest and cheapest rim tape is electrician's tape. It's usually found in packs of four in automotive shops and is just the right width for a mountain bike rim.

Threads

The threads on spokes are regular righthand. So when viewed from the threaded end inside the rim – tightening is clockwise and slackening is anti-clockwise.

Rim splitting

Badly worn braking surfaces can lead to the bead section of the rim bursting apart under the force of an inflated tyre. Check your rims regularly for cracks on the braking surface and around the spoke bed.

Spoke key

Always use a good quality spoke key that is the correct size. A badly-fitting spoke key will do more harm than good.

Which spoke?

If you're not sure which side to adjust, grab two spokes on one side and squeeze them together to see which way the rim moves.

Dents

A dent doesn't necessarily mean the end of the wheel. So long as it trues up straight and the dent doesn't interfere with the brakes, or makes the tyre touch the brakes, then it can be used just that little bit longer.

Wheel building

Building wheels from scratch is a skilled job, and is not part of everyday maintenance – so it isn't shown in this book.

A dent doesn't necessarily
mean the end of the wheel.

MAKING REPAIRS OUT ON THE TRAIL

Introduction

Things always go wrong at the wrong time don't they! Just when you're enjoying yourself, suddenly... Twa-thang! You're being overtaken by your own rear mech.

Usually you suffer not much more than a puncture during a day's riding, but when something major does go wrong, you're better off knowing what to do about it rather than having to walk home (and it always starts raining just after something goes wrong).

Here are a few tips and bodges to get you home, back to the car, the phone box, or whatever.

Trail repair kit

INNER TUBE -it's far quicker to replace a punctured tube than repair it. Make sure the valve fits the hole in your rim

20P PIECE - if all else fails and you have to call the cavalry

PATCH KIT- Glue, sandpaper, big and small patches, chalk

SPOKE KEY- If your multi tool doesn't include one. Make sure it's the correct size

TYRE LEVERS- get plastic ones, metal ones can damage the tube

PUMP - make sure that the adaptor is correct for your inner tubes either presta or schrader

MULTI - TOOLS These combine many useful tools in one lightweight package. You should carry a minimum of; 4, 5, 6mm allen keys, 8, 9, 10mm spanners (or adjustable), screw driver, a chain tool and a socket or allen key that fits your cranks

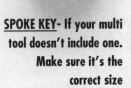

1. Quick release crank bolts

Use extractor crank bolts such as Sugino Autex, Syncros Crank-O-Matics, or Shimano One-key Releases (if you can find some). If the chain does get well and truly stuck behind the granny ring and the frame, you'll be able to pull the crank off without having to carry a crank puller. Grease the threads of the bolts thoroughly and also grease the top face of the bolt that pushes against the extractor ring. Once you arrange for as little friction as possible in these areas, your cranks will come off using a regular Allen key and brute force.

2. Broken spokes

If you break a spoke on the drive side of the rear wheel you can either wrap it around the spoke next to it, or if it breaks too short, you can use a Pamir Engineering Hyper Cracker. It's a neat little tool that allows you to remove and refit a Shimano Hyperglide lockring. After removing the skewer you refit the wheel in the frame and pedal the crank, which loosens the lockring. Remove the wheel, then the sprockets, and you have access to the drive side spokes to remove the remains of the broken spoke. Refit the sprockets, lock-ring, and tool, and put the wheel back in the bike. Put the bike on its wheels and roll it backwards to tighten the lockring.

3. Damaged tyres

Cuts in the side walls of a tyre don't happen too often, but when they do the results can be dangerous. First fit a new tube, or repair the current one. There are several ways of repairing the hole in the sidewall. If you are carrying tools wrapped in a rag wrap the rag around the part of the inner tube next to the hole in the tyre. This stops that part of the tube sticking out through the hole. If you don't have a rag then look for anything that can be put between the tyre and tube. Fresh vegetation often has a few strong leaves to spare, stuff them inside the tyre to cover the hole and inflate it just enough to let you ride. Anything will do, even the lining of a pocket from your clothes or the sleeve of a T-shirt.

4. Trashed wheels

A severely bent wheel is useless, and you'll never get it back straight or serviceable with a spoke key. The only thing you can do is to straighten it enough so that it will pass through the frame and allow the bike to be ridden. Place the wheel on the floor and stand on the offending bent sections until it is straight enough to do the job. Initial straightening is best done by hitting the bent section of rim against the floor, a tree or a rock. Somehow this shock treatment seems to get the wheel straighter,

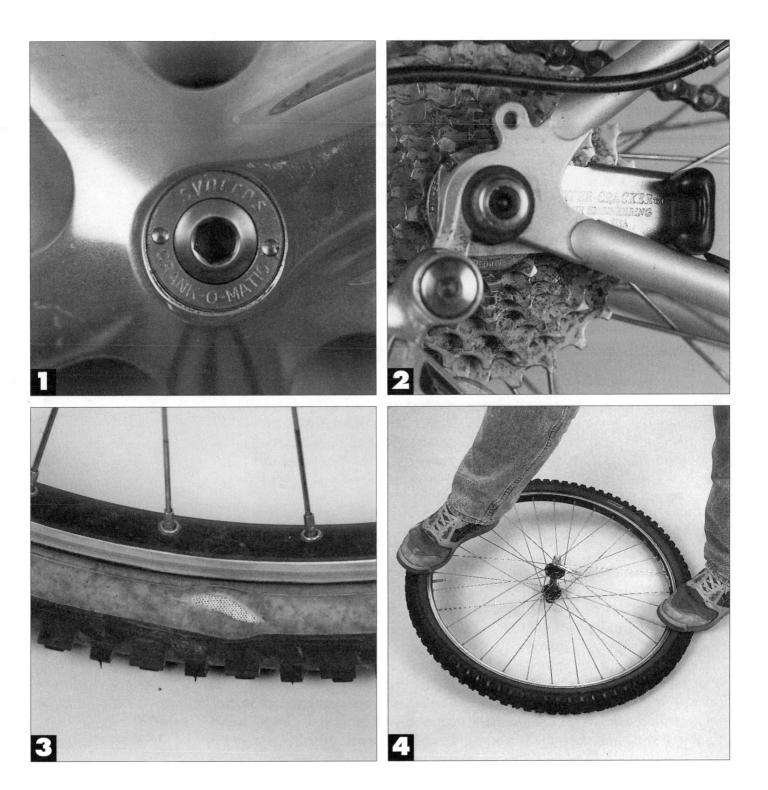

quicker. Rim and spokes should be replaced as soon as possible.

5. Bent mech hanger

Small falls often bend the rear mech hanger, but don't damage the rear mech. This leaves the rear mech out of line with the sprockets and your gears just won't want to know. On a steel frame you can gently bend the hanger back more or less straight with a spanner (the adjustable type is best). With an aluminium frame it isn't wise to attempt this because the material will more than likely fail when you try to bend it back. On most aluminium frames the mech hanger is replaceable, so it's wise to carry a replacement, and the tools necessary, if you are riding in the wilds.

6. Dead rear mech

Rear mechs break, but it doesn't mean the bike is unridable. Split the chain and run it out of the rear mech. You can either leave the rear mech on the frame, or take it off and carry it with you. Run the chain on the middle chainring and over one of the rear sprockets (choose a gear that suits the terrain you have to ride home on), then join the chain as tight as you can. The bike will now be ridable – it might be hard work on the hills but it's still quicker and more enjoyable than pushing.

7. Loose headset

You need a big spanner to adjust and lock up a conventional headset. Carrying something this size out on the trail is out of the question (unless you are on an expedition), so here's a tip that will refit a loose headset at least tighter than you can achieve by hand. Loosen the top locknut off and adjust the lower one by hand until most or all of the bearing play has gone. It helps if you rock the bike back and forth with the front brake on when you tighten the lower one. Then tighten the top locknut down by hand as tight as you can get it. Wrap a leather toe strap around the top locknut and pull it tight. It works like a band brake, the harder you pull it, the tighter it grabs the nut. Of course, this is useless advice if you don't have a leather toe strap!

8. Bent chainrings

Bashed chainrings are probably the most common 'disaster' when out riding. However, it's usually only the large chainring that gets bent, and straightening it isn't too hard. Place an adjustable spanner on the chainring as shown and bend it back as straight as you can get it. If you don't have anything to straighten it with, bash it with a rock or something – remember, the idea is to make the bike ridable and get home again.

Hints 'n' tips

Tools

Roll your tools up in a rag, fold the ends of the rag over and tie the whole thing up in a leather toe strap (because you can use it to tighten a headset, right!). The tools are kept safe, clean, and together, and the rag can be used for cleaning hands and bike and to stop the inner tube sticking out through a torn tyre.

Lightweight mini screwdriver

Cut the end off a screwdriver (Phillips No2 for Shimano stuff) so that you're left with a miniature screwdriver with no handle (about 50mm/2inch is just right). Cut a slot in the sawn off end big enough to take the edge of a twenty pence piece and put them both in with your other tools. When you need to use the screwdriver turn it with the 20p in the slot – when you need to use the 20p, put it in the telephone and call for help! For a more substantial screwdriver, file two flats at the end so you can use a spanner to turn it.

Telephones

If you do get stuck with an unridable bike and no money, you can still call for help. Dial the operator (dial 100) and ask for a reverse charge call to the number you wish to dial.

Puncture stuff

As a bare minimum, carry at least one spare tube, a couple of patches and glue, and a pump of some kind. Gas canister inflation devices are fine if you are racing but are a bit of a waste if you're just out riding. Don't worry about your friends having to wait while you fix a flat, if they're really friends they'll come and help. If you do puncture and don't have a spare tube or puncture repair kit you can tie a knot in the inner tube so that the part with the hole is in the knot. Inflate the tube pretty hard to help tighten the knot, then deflate it and put it back in the tyre. Limp on home with a soft but functional tyre.

Snapped bars

If you snap your bars – and haven't hurt yourself too bad – here's what to do. If the bars haven't snapped off completely, finish the job and snap them off! Find a stick that will fit tightly inside each end of the two parts – use a rock to hit it into the stem part, then hit the rest of the bar with the grip, brake, shifter

JARGON

ALLEN KEY – hexagonal-shaped rod bent at 90° that fits into the head of an Allen bolt. Almost every bike uses Allen bolts.

DERAILLEUR – the mechanism that pushes the chain from one sprocket to the next. The front derailleur shifts the chain on the front chainrings and the rear derailleur shifts the chain on the rear gear sprockets.

FRONT MECH – the front derailleur.

HEADSET – the bearing assembly between the fork steerer and the headtube of the frame.

HYPERGLIDE – the brand name given to Shimano rear gear sprockets that have profiled teeth and special 'shift ramps'.

QUICK RELEASE/QR – a lever mechanism for fastening the wheel quickly and easily into the frame/forks. The QR runs through the wheel axle, and when the lever is closed it applies force between its ends in much the same way as tightening wheel nuts

REAR MECH – see derailleur.

on, on to the stick. It may take a few good hits but at least you'll be able to steer the bike home slowly.

Crank bolts

Loose crank bolts are a pain but now that most Shimano crank bolts require 8mm Allen keys they are a lot easier to tighten while out riding. The problem now is that you have to carry an 8mm Allen key – which is usually large and heavy. To remedy this cut the end off an 8mm Allen key (so you have a one inch Allen key with no bend) and use the 8mm spanner you should be carrying to turn it.

Alternatively, you can buy aftermarket bolts (such as those manufactured by Royce UK) which require a 6mm Allen key. Standard and Shimano Low Profile compatible bolts are available in either steel or titanium.

MTB ANATOMY

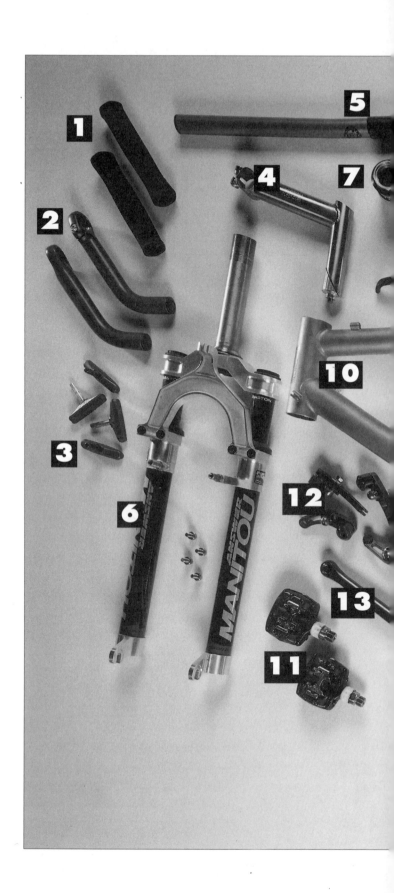

1) Grips

2) Bar ends

3) Brake blocks

4) Stem

5) Bar sleeve and bar

6) Suspension forks

7) Headset

8) XTR brake/shifter assemblies

9) Cable yoke

10) Head tube

11) SPD pedals

12) Cantilever brake arm

13) Crank arm

14) Chainrings

15) Spider

16) Bottom bracket

17) Chain

18) Cassette

19) Quick release skewers

20) Rear derailleur

21) Front hub

22) Rear hub

23) Seat post

24) Marin Lite TI saddle

25) Marin Lite 2.1 tyre

26) Brake pivot

27) Wheelsmith spokes

28) Aluminium nipples

29) Mavic 230 rims

30) Inner tube

31) Front Derailleur

32) Seat post bolt

33) Top tube

34) Drop out

35) Cable guide

36) Seat Tube

37) Seat stay bridge

38) Chainstay

39) Down Tube

40) Bottom bracket shell

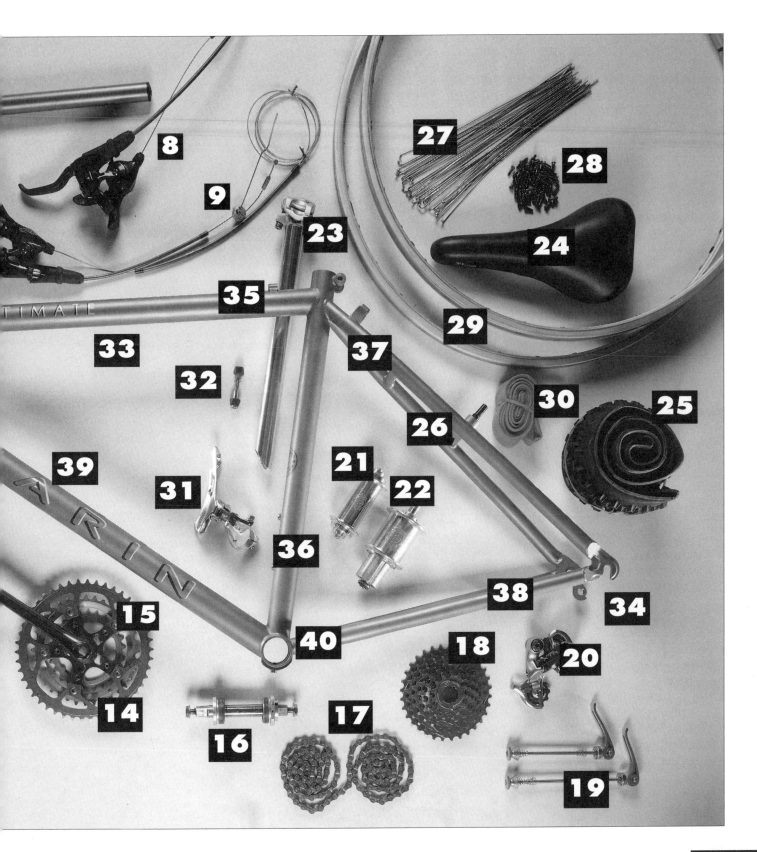

INDEX

Author's Acknowledgements

The author would like to thank:

John Stevenson, Rich Howat, Brant Richards, Russell Fisher, Miggy,

Paul Vincent, Mark Severs, Lloyd Townsend, Helen Sudell, Maria Bowers,

Justin Loretz, Chris Hague, Peter Moss

Picture Acknowledgements

Front cover : Pete Canning

Frontispiece: Bob Smith

All other photographs courtesy of Rob Scott and Pete Canning